SARAH C

LAND YOUR NEXT L&D ROLE

Creating a Career That Works for You

atd
PRESS
Alexandria, VA

© 2025 ASTD DBA the Association for Talent Development (ATD)
All rights reserved. Printed in the United States of America.

28 27 26 25   1 2 3 4 5

No part of this publication may be reproduced, distributed, or transmitted in any form or by any means, including photocopying, recording, information storage and retrieval systems, or other electronic or mechanical methods, without the prior written permission of the publisher, except in the case of brief quotations embodied in critical reviews and certain other noncommercial uses permitted by copyright law. For permission requests, please go to copyright.com, or contact Copyright Clearance Center (CCC), 222 Rosewood Drive, Danvers, MA 01923 (tele-phone: 978.750.8400; fax: 978.646.8600).

ATD Press is an internationally renowned source of insightful and practical information on talent development, training, and professional development.

ATD Press
1640 King Street
Alexandria, VA 22314 USA

Ordering information: Books published by ATD Press can be purchased by visiting ATD's website at td.org/books or by calling 800.628.2783 or 703.683.8100.

Library of Congress Control Number: 2024950311

ISBN-10: 1-95715-784-4
ISBN-13: 978-1-95715-784-9
e-ISBN: 978-1-95715-785-6

ATD Press Editorial Staff
Director: Sarah Halgas
Manager: Melissa Jones
Content Manager, Career Development: Mallory Flynn
Developmental Editor: Jack Harlow
Text Designer: Shirley E.M. Raybuck
Cover Designer: Rose Richey

Text Layout: Kathleen Dyson

Printed by BR Printers, San Jose, CA

Contents

Introduction 1

Part 1: Laying the Foundation for Your L&D Career
    Chapter 1: The 4 L&D Career Success Codes 9
    Chapter 2: Setting Goals and Creating Your L&D Career Timeline 19
    Chapter 3: Discovering Your L&D Career Confidence and Competence 35
    Chapter 4: Finding Your L&D Niche 49
    Chapter 5: Motivation, Mindsets, and Habits 61

Part 2: Positioning Yourself in the L&D Market
    Chapter 6: Career Leveling, Placement, and Quantifying Your Value 79
    Chapter 7: Creating Your Niche-Aligned Resume and Cover Letter 91
    Chapter 8: Building Your L&D Personal Brand 109

Part 3: Networking and Building Relationships
    Chapter 9: The 3 Ls of Networking 129
    Chapter 10: Constructing Your L&D Network Ecosystem 139
    Chapter 11: Having Impactful Networking Conversations 151

Part 4: Mastering the L&D Job Search Process
    Chapter 12: Interview Preparedness 163
    Chapter 13: Preparing for a Scheduled Interview 177
    Chapter 14: Post Interview: How to Stand Out 187
    Chapter 15: Navigating Career Rejection 193

Part 5: Thriving in Your New L&D Role
    Chapter 16: You've Landed Your Dream L&D Role—What's Next? 201

Afterword 207
Acknowledgments 209
Resources 213
References 215
Index 223
About the Author 233
About ATD 235

Introduction

"Change is inevitable. But transformation is a choice."
—Heather Ash Amara

My L&D career almost ended before it even began.

Like many millennials, I started working in my teens. I've always had a propensity toward the service and sales industries—from working in restaurants to phone sales to retail to fundraising. I found myself drawn toward helping people, but like most 20 year olds, I had no idea what that meant for my long-term career.

I decided to study psychology at the University of Central Florida. I enjoyed my classes but was struggling to pay rent. My apartment community offered a rent discount as an employment perk, so my mom encouraged me to apply for a sales associate position. Begrudgingly (because I thought I knew everything and didn't need my mom's advice—spoiler alert, mom is always right), I applied for the job and within a few weeks was hired full-time.

Prior to this, I'd only held part-time, odds-and-ends jobs, so I'd never experienced a formal onboarding process. I had no idea what to expect as I walked into the corporate office on my first day. My orientation was a whirlwind—learning about the real estate industry, the company's core values, and what had made the organization successful for the past few decades. Divisional leaders who started as associates shared their journeys and success stories. We ate lunch together, learned about everyone's backgrounds, and shared pictures of the properties we were going to work at—promising to visit one another in the coming weeks. We laughed, we learned, and we developed an overwhelming sense of connection to one another and the organization—all in just eight short hours. More than 15 years later, I can *still* think back and feel that sense of excitement coursing through me as I left the office to begin my new career.

As the onboarding process continued—complete with job shadowing, mentorship, and on-the-job training—I became more and more confident in my new role, very quickly rising to the top of the sales boards for not only our region, but the entire country. I immersed myself in learning sales techniques, becoming a product expert, and uncovering how to deliver the best possible client experience. For the first time in my life, I felt I was on the right career path, with each step carefully laid out in front of me.

That was, until I experienced my first in-person training session.

I'll never forget the moment I first saw Steve Wunch. A regional trainer at the time, Steve was responsible for hosting the company's sales rallies for regional sales associates. This quarterly event gave us the chance to celebrate the past quarter and engage in a half-day of learning experiences to propel us into the next quarter.

When Steve got on the microphone, the energy in the room became electric. All eyes were on him—everyone was engaged and actively participating with the sales topic he was presenting. He made us laugh, he challenged us, and he left us feeling confident in applying this new information back on the job. I can't remember what we learned about that day—it might have been closing techniques or objection handling. What I do remember was the feeling I had the moment Steve stepped on the stage. I felt a shift that would change the trajectory of my career when I realized that this, what Steve was doing, was what I wanted to do one day.

And while I wish I could tell you I became a trainer overnight (which I did, a few years later), that experience only marked the *beginning* of my journey toward training.

I left the rally and went back to work. Because I kept exceeding my sales targets, the company asked me to help train and mentor new sales associates. I eventually joined a competing organization and was promoted into a leadership role. As a sales manager, I spent most of my time hosting sales training sessions for my teams, creating process documents and manuals, recording videos on how to use new technologies, and providing one-on-one coaching and mentorship. Without even recognizing it, my L&D career was starting to take shape—just without the formal title, training, or experience.

Then, I enrolled in a two-day leadership development program that my company's newly formed learning and leadership department was piloting. Seeing the facilitator, Genevieve, command the room in the same way Steve had done at that rally years earlier reignited my fire for a career in training.

At the end of the two days, I approached Genevieve and the head of the learning and leadership team, Steven. I shared my desire to get into training, asking for their advice and if there was anything I could do to start moving the needle forward in my L&D career journey. They shared a speaking look, turned back to me, and asked me if I'd be open to becoming a software trainer. Without hesitation, I said yes. This time I became a trainer, overnight.

Of course, I was now doing software training *in addition* to my sales manager role. But the more I immersed myself in teaching and training, the more I knew I wanted to make it my full-time career.

And then it happened. The weekly company-wide internal job posting email hit my inbox, and at the very top was an opening for a corporate trainer. This was it! It was time to fully transition into learning and development. I was jumping for joy as I read through the job description, only to have my heart plummet when I saw this line: *Bachelor's degree required.*

A few months after beginning my career in sales, I had decided to withdraw from college. I realized I wasn't passionate about studying psychology and found it challenging to work a full-time job while attending school. At the time, it was the middle of the 2008 financial crisis, and my friends were having trouble finding work even with their degrees. So, I made the decision to focus entirely on my career—and that choice had served me well, up until that moment. Once I saw those words written so plainly on the job description, I was devastated. I didn't qualify—so I didn't apply and tucked away my dreams of an L&D career.

A few weeks later, Jeanette, the L&D coordinator at the time (who went on to become one of the most talented instructional design professionals I know), pulled me aside and said Steven wanted to meet with me in his office. "This is it," I thought, gutted. "They filled the corporate trainer position and are letting me go."

As I sat in the chair on the other side of Steven's desk, I was not prepared for the question he asked me. "Why didn't you apply for the corporate trainer position?" In fact, I think I nearly fainted, but the shame I'd been harboring about dropping out of college quickly brought me back to reality.

Looking down at my fidgeting hands, I said quietly, "I really wanted to, but the role requires a college degree, and I don't have one."

Steven shifted in his seat and then he let out a bark of laughter. What?! As if the situation could get any worse! Someone I greatly admired, who I would do anything to work for, was laughing at me.

But he wasn't laughing at me; he was laughing with a sense of relief—relief for me. "You've already been doing the job as a sales manager and systems trainer," he said with a big smile on his face. "I'd much prefer to have someone who knows the company, the culture, and is a subject matter expert over someone with a degree."

He saw what I didn't, and at that time couldn't, see—my transferable skill set and how it prepared me for my dream role. To Steven, it wasn't about the degrees I didn't have or the titles I'd held—the unique set of skills I'd gained from my experience made me the right person for the role.

After that conversation, I formally applied for the job and went through the interview process. Within weeks, I officially transitioned to my role as a corporate trainer. A few years later, I became the company's first director of corporate training. Then, I went back to school for a degree in organizational leadership and learning before leading the L&D functions at three more organizations. Eventually, I decided to embark on an entrepreneurial journey to help L&D professionals find, land, and thrive in the L&D career of their dreams, just as I had.

My journey wasn't straightforward—there were twists and turns, I suffered from imposter syndrome and self-doubt, and there was even a several month stint when I left the field completely. In fact, as I write this book, I'm in the thick of another professional transformation. In many ways, putting pen to paper is cathartic. It's been a self-reflective way to share the experiments, models, and tools that more than 1,000 of my clients have used in the last four years and that I've used over the past few months.

This book is designed to be transformative and to guide you on your L&D career journey, no matter the stage you're in. You are in the right place if you are:
- Just beginning your L&D career or considering a transition into L&D
- Ready to advance in your L&D career or try a new type of role inside the field
- Realizing your work environment no longer aligns with your core values and are looking for a new role inside a new company
- Looking to set yourself up for success inside your current organization in preparation for a promotion
- Recently laid off, unemployed, or underemployed and looking to find your next stable L&D role

We're in an incredible time for learning and development. The artificial intelligence (AI) revolution is upon us, and while many fear it will take away jobs, I believe that it's going to create so many new opportunities for our field. After decades, we're finally being invited to the table inside many organizations, and we're leading the charge internally on skill development and talent mobility. L&D budgets are growing, even during recent periods of economic uncertainty, and we're seeing more and more traditional and nontraditional L&D roles hit the job market than ever before.

There has never been a better time to invest in your own L&D career than right now.

This book will challenge many ideas and practices you've learned about finding and building a career in talent development. It will require you to have an open mind and, frankly, an open heart. It will also require you to reflect on your career so far and envision what's possible for you in the future. It will test you again and again, but in return, you'll gain clarity, confidence, and competence.

You picked up this book for a reason. I encourage you to use it to its fullest to rewrite the narrative of your career and transform it into the L&D career of your dreams.

PART 1
Laying the Foundation for Your L&D Career

Chapter 1
The 4 L&D Career Success Codes

"I never dreamed about success, I worked for it."
—Estee Lauder

If you picked up this book, you're probably looking for the best strategy to find and land your next L&D role. Everyone (and their mother and brother and sister) has likely shared their strategies to "guarantee" you'll land a new role. I can also bet you're feeling a little overwhelmed by the thought of "Frankensteining" all those strategies into something that actually works for you.

I'll let you in on a secret: There is no one-size-fits-all strategy.

We all have different lived experiences, personalities, ways of working, and communication styles. While one person thrives in an environment where they are meeting and connecting with new people every day, someone else may find that utterly terrifying. Where one person might successfully create original content to land their dream role, another person may find success through a referral from a small community of like-minded peers.

The adage "one person's trash is another person's treasure," can also be applied to the strategy you adopt to find and land your dream L&D role. What worked for someone on the internet may not work for you—in fact, it could actually hinder your progress. The more you take bits and pieces from other people's career transition strategy, the further away you'll be from what feels good to you. If it doesn't feel aligned, or feels forced, there's a high likelihood you won't find success in that strategy.

The ABCDs of Career Success

So, we've established that each person's approach should be unique to their own experience. But what about their strategy? As I've coached clients through their job searches, I've found that certain patterns of activities led my clients to land higher quality roles in a significantly shorter timeframe than the average L&D job seeker. And, the more they align these specific strategies to their own unique experiences, the more successful they are.

I call these strategies the L&D Career Success Codes, or the ABCDs. Let's take a look at each one:

- **A (alignment).** This success code involves gaining clarity about your career goals. You want to determine what role is right for you, based on your skills and interests (or your L&D niche, which we'll define in chapter 4). You're also identifying the type of company values to target (more on this in chapters 3 and 4) and creating career transition materials, such as your resume, cover letter or CV, and portfolio (if needed) that speak to your ideal role.
- **B (branding).** This success code involves creating a personal and professional brand and crafting your story. Your brand is what others say about you when you're not in the room and it can work passively for you, whereas other success codes require more active attention. You'll focus on optimizing your LinkedIn profile, website, content, and portfolio to reflect what you want, how you want to do it, and who you want to do it for.
- **C (community).** This success code goes beyond networking for the sake of networking; here the focus is on spending time intentionally building community around your L&D niche. It is all about being in the room where it happens and finding people you can leverage, learn from, and lean on. You may want to join associations, group coaching programs, memberships, LinkedIn groups, and so on. Remember, it's not about the quantity of people you are connected with, but rather, the quality.

- **D (development).** This success code has two subcategories:
  - *Professional development* involves doing a gap analysis so you can start to understand where you need to upskill and create a plan to do so, without overdeveloping yourself. You'll want to focus on developing key skills, rather than collecting courses and certifications for the sake of having them.
  - *Personal development* involves focusing on your mindset and developing sustainable habits, hobbies, systems, and strategies to build your resilience and improve your relationship with yourself. This might be the most underrated piece of the success codes. Without a direct focus on your own internal belief systems and self-care, the process for developing into your next role will be long, arduous, and unstable.

When it comes time to adopt the ABCDs, there are three *very important* things to remember:

- You don't have to operate evenly in all four success codes.
- You don't have to focus on all four success codes at the same time.
- Your success codes strategy can (and most likely will) evolve as you progress through the job search.

The Success Codes in Action

Let's take a look at three real-life examples:

> **Meet Marylynne:** When Marylynne (a former educator) came to me, she was feeling defeated, not like herself, and very "communitied"-out. A member of several L&D career transition communities, Marylynne had fallen into the trap of applying every piece of one-off advice to her career transition. So, when we started working together, she opted to focus on the alignment success code. Marylynne initially put 90 percent of her effort into finding her L&D niche and developing a niche-aligned resume and cover letter. Then, once her resume and cover letter authentically represented her unique set of skills, interests, and values, she shifted her strategy to focus more on her personal brand and aligning that to her newly discovered niche (Figure 1-1).

Figure 1-1. Marylynne's Career Transition Strategy

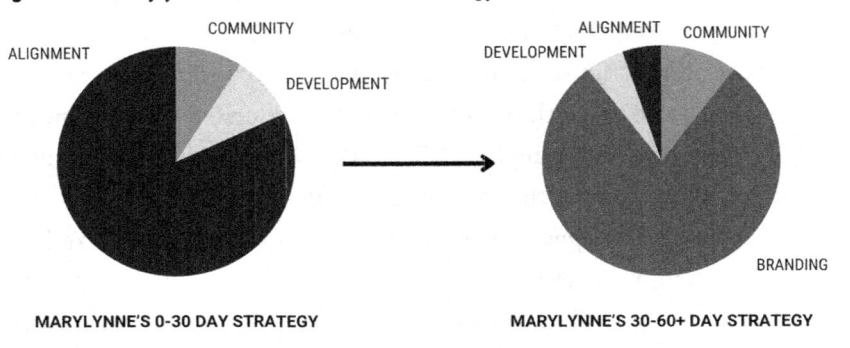

MARYLYNNE'S 0-30 DAY STRATEGY

MARYLYNNE'S 30-60+ DAY STRATEGY

Meet Erin: When Erin (a former learning program director) and I first started working together, she was trying to find a new job after being part of a tech company's reduction of force. Despite having dual master's degrees and decades of experience, her rejection letters were piling up and her confidence was taking a major dip. She had resorted to applying to any and all roles—including ones she was overqualified for. Once we began working together, we identified Erin's unique L&D niche and focused her strategy on rebuilding her confidence through personal development (Figure 1-2). Erin also realized that her network didn't quite align with her niche, so she set out to create a community of people with the same career passions who she could leverage, learn from, and lean on. Eventually this network led Erin to a referral—which turned into a dream job offer.

Figure 1-2. Erin's Career Transition Strategy

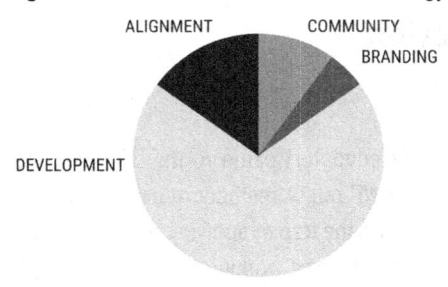

ERIN'S STRATEGY (NO CHANGE)

Meet Rebecca: Before Rebecca (a former university senior lecturer) and I began working together, she was hiding parts of her skill set to showcase what she thought hiring managers wanted to see—effectively blending in with every other candidate out there. When we peeled back the layers to determine what skills she actually wanted to use in her next role, Rebecca realized she wanted to use both her artistic skills (she's a digital artist) and her research background (she was an MIT doctoral researcher). By combining those two skill sets, we found her L&D niche and crafted a resume around it. Rebecca quickly landed a first-round interview for her dream L&D job, thanks in part to her unique collection of skills. As she progressed through the interview process, Rebecca switched gears to focus on her own development (Figure 1-3). Leaning heavily on her research background, Rebecca decided to grow her skill sets in L&D data analytics and visualization. A few months later, she had two job offers in hand and landed the L&D role of her dreams.

Figure 1-3. Rebecca's Career Transition Strategy

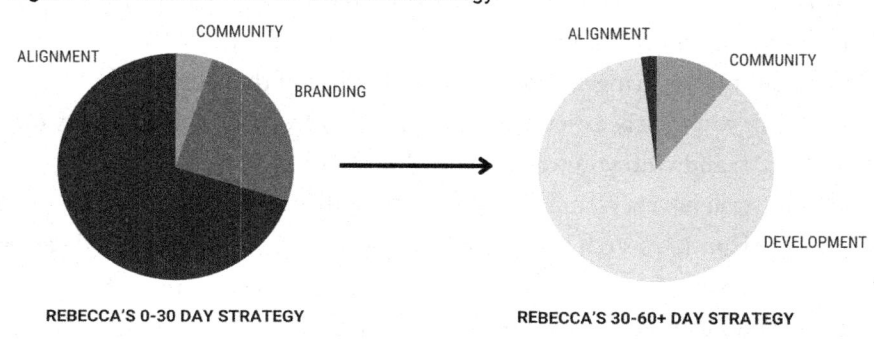

REBECCA'S 0-30 DAY STRATEGY — COMMUNITY, ALIGNMENT, BRANDING

REBECCA'S 30-60+ DAY STRATEGY — ALIGNMENT, COMMUNITY, DEVELOPMENT

As you can see, strategies may shift over time or stay consistent, depending on each individual's situation. Marylynne's and Rebecca's strategies both shifted around the 30-day mark, whereas Erin's stayed mostly the same throughout her L&D career transition journey.

Marylynne had been putting together a piecemeal strategy for over a year before we started working together, so she needed that initial focus on alignment. She took the time necessary to find out what she actually wanted, rather than focusing on what her old community thought she should want. Once Marylynne felt aligned, she could focus on what most excited her—building a personal brand around her newly aligned L&D niche.

Rebecca was still relatively new to the career transition journey, so she didn't know what she didn't know and was falling into the trap of blending in. We needed to shift her focus to understanding how all parts of her skill set could come together as a unique niche. Once Rebecca determined her niche, she was able to identify a few small skills gaps and create a professional development plan to close them.

Erin's strategy remained relatively unchanged during our entire time working together. We knew the key to success would be building her confidence incrementally so she could believe and articulate with ease the value she would bring to her dream L&D role.

How to Know Where to Start

These are just a few examples of how my clients have successfully used the ABCDs as a framework to land their L&D roles. The possibilities are endless for how you could use them in your own career journey.

If you're wondering where to start, ask yourself these questions:
- Can you clearly articulate what you want to do next, how you want to do it, and who you want to do it for?
- Do you have a resume that aligns with that vision?
- Do your job search materials showcase your skills, interests, and values?

If you answered no to any of those questions, I recommend starting with the alignment success code. Without alignment, it will be challenging to understand and use the rest of the success codes.

If you answered yes to those questions, you're ready to explore the other success codes. Here are a few more questions to help clarify your direction:
- On a scale from 1 to 10, how confident are you in your ability to find and land your next L&D role?
    - If you answered lower than a seven, I encourage you to explore the chapters on the personal development success code (particularly chapters 2, 3, and 5). If you don't have confidence in your own abilities, it will be difficult for others, especially those in a hiring position, to be confident in your abilities.
- What five words do you want people to think of when they look at your LinkedIn profile, website, blog, or other online presence? When you're not in the room, what five words do you want people to say about the work you do? Does your current personal brand reflect this?
    - If you aren't sure or don't think your personal brand reflects what you want others to see, you might start by focusing on the branding success code and its related chapters. Your online

presence serves as a passive and relatively easy way to attract and receive job opportunities. You want to make sure that anyone passing by your brand will clearly understand what you bring to the table and what you're capable of doing for their organization.
- Do you have a group of L&D peers you can leverage, learn from, and lean on?
    - If you answered no I suggest focusing on the community success code and its related chapters. Build a network of people who share a similar alignment with you. This can be as simple as fostering a handful of strong one-on-one connections, finding a talent development networking group, or joining your local ATD chapter.
- Have you performed a skills gap assessment on yourself recently? Do you know which areas you'll need to upskill and develop to reach your L&D career goals?
    - If you answered no I suggest focusing on creating a professional development plan by focusing on the development success code and its related chapters (particularly chapter 3). Remember, a collection of arbitrary certifications and courses is not the same as aligning your specific areas of focus with your L&D career goals. You want to be intentional with this area, especially because it requires an investment of your time, money, and energy.

Depending on how you answered these questions, you may want to focus on one, two, three, or even all four success codes. If one or two areas are really calling to you, I encourage you to start there first, and then work your way through the others. Use Table 1-1 as a quick guide to target the chapters that are most relevant to your success codes of choice.

Table 1-1. L&D Career Success Codes: Chapter Matrix

Success Codes	2	3	4	5	6	7	8	9
Alignment	x	x	x	x	x	x		
Branding						x	x	
Community							x	x
Development	x	x		x				

Success Codes	10	11	12	13	14	15	16
Alignment			x	x	x	x	x
Branding	x		x	x	x		x
Community	x	x					x
Development	x						x

Another way to look at using the success codes is time allocation. If you've decided to focus on multiple success codes, you may want to start by assigning percentages to each one. Let's return to Marylynne's strategy.

> Marylynne did not have unlimited hours to spend focusing on finding her next L&D role. In fact, because of her current full-time job, she only had about an hour a day (and sometimes less) to dedicate to her career transition.
>
> We worked out a plan for Marylynne's first 30 days that focused about 80 percent on alignment and about 10 percent each on community and development. The resulting time allocation typically looked like this:
> - Total time: 1 hour/day (7 hours total)
>   - Alignment: 5.5 hours
>   - Community: 30–60 minutes
>   - Development: 30–60 minutes
>
> Once she was confident in her alignment, we shifted her strategy to focus more on branding. Marylynne's success code allotment shifted accordingly to about 75 percent branding, 10 percent development, and 5 percent for alignment and community:
> - Total time: 1 hour/day (7 hours total)
>   - Branding: 5.25 hours
>   - Development: 30–60 minutes
>   - Alignment: 20–30 minutes
>   - Community: 20–30 minutes

As you can see from Marylynne's example, using the success codes to properly allot your most precious career transition resource—your time—will help you unlock success in a quicker, more streamlined fashion.

How to Use This Book

In this book, I've labeled each chapter with the corresponding success codes so you can focus on the areas that feel most aligned to you, when you need them most. However, depending on where you are in your journey, there are a few different ways to maximize this book's effectiveness. Let's look closer at how this book can help you achieve your L&D career goals when you're in different stages of the journey:

- **You're currently in a passive job search or just starting to think about what's next for you and your L&D career.** If you have an elongated timeframe (more than six months) or no timeframe, I encourage you to read this book from start to finish. Each concept and chapter builds on the next; by going in order and practicing the activities, you'll create an incredibly strong launch pad on which you can ignite your engine and go after your dream L&D role.
- **You're actively searching for your next L&D role and need a bit of a jump start.** If you've already dipped your toes into the L&D job market, it's a great time to revisit your answers to the questions from earlier in this chapter to identify a good starting point. Once you determine how to allocate your time, I encourage you to seek out the chapters for the relevant success codes and apply the best practices you learn in each.
- **You're deep in the trenches and need to land your next L&D role ASAP!** Before you let the desperation sink all the way in, first and foremost, take a deep breath. Once you've done that, take inventory of what you've done and what's moved the needle for you (for example, landing interviews from referrals, receiving a cold message from a recruiter on LinkedIn, or moving on to a second-round interview). How can you amplify what's already working? For example, if your referrals have led to interviews, you may want to start by leaning into

the community success code before diving into something else. Once you amplify what is working, you can take inventory of what isn't and shift your focus to those success codes.

What's Next? Getting Started

A few things to reflect on as we embark on this L&D career journey together:
- Have you been operating strategically from a place of alignment? Or have you been combining piecemeal snippets of advice from person after person?
- What success code do you think needs the most attention? Which ones come next and at what approximate percentage?
- What is your timeframe for finding a new career? Based on your sense of urgency, how should you start or reframe your journey?

Chapter 2
Setting Goals and Creating Your L&D Career Timeline

"Sometimes we are so focused on what we want, we miss the things we need." —Anonymous

When you start thinking about your next career move, it's easy to immediately want to set an actionable goal, or goals, so you have something specific to aim for. In a society that is constantly demanding SMART goals, it's important to remember that setting goals is about more than making them specific, measurable, realistic, and so on. You want to get to the core of your career desires—starting with your needs and intentions—and use that to craft strategically aligned goals (Figure 2-1).

Figure 2-1. Needs > Intentions > Goals

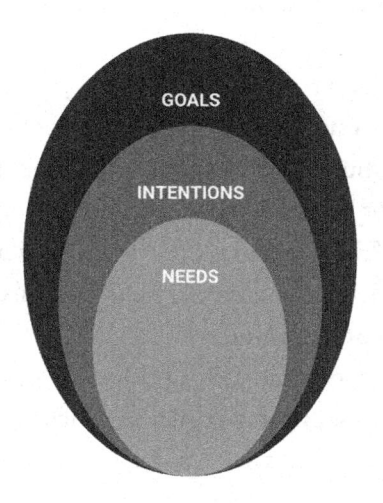

Needs-First Approach to Goal Setting

When you center your goals around your wants, you are placing certain specific criteria around *how* your needs must be fulfilled. But how do you know what specific criteria is warranted to fulfill those needs if you haven't established them?

Think of the last goal you set for yourself. How much thought went into your core *needs* when you set that goal? Or did you base it more arbitrarily on your *wants*?

> **Meet Brittany:** When Brittany first came to me for L&D career coaching, she had been recently laid off from her curriculum designer position. While she wasn't completely happy in her previous role, she wasn't expecting to be laid off and wasn't prepared for the new career journey. Once she dusted herself off from the shock of the layoff, she set a goal for herself: Land a new L&D role as quickly as possible.

Based on what we've discussed so far, do you see any problems with Brittany's goal? It wasn't rooted in *how* she could fulfill her career needs. This left her feeling her overwhelmed and disappointed every time she thought about it—weighing her down instead of fueling her.

To identify your career needs, we're going to use (and iterate on) Maslow's Hierarchy of Needs to create a full-circle definition of your L&D career transition pillars.

Maslow's Hierarchy of Needs (Figure 2-2) is "a theory of psychology explaining human motivation based on the pursuit of different levels of needs. The theory states that humans are motivated to fulfill their needs in a hierarchical order. This order begins with the most basic needs before moving on to more advanced needs" (CFI Team n.d.). Maslow's hierarchy is often used by the human resources field as a marker of how to ensure employees feel a sense of belonging inside an organization.

While Maslow argued that each need builds on the next, others argue there is little evidence to support the order in which the hierarchy is presented. What research has shown, however, is that the fulfillment of these specific needs is strongly correlated with happiness (University of Illinois 2011). What good are your L&D career goals if they don't lead to a semblance of happiness?

Figure 2-2. Maslow's Hierarchy of Needs

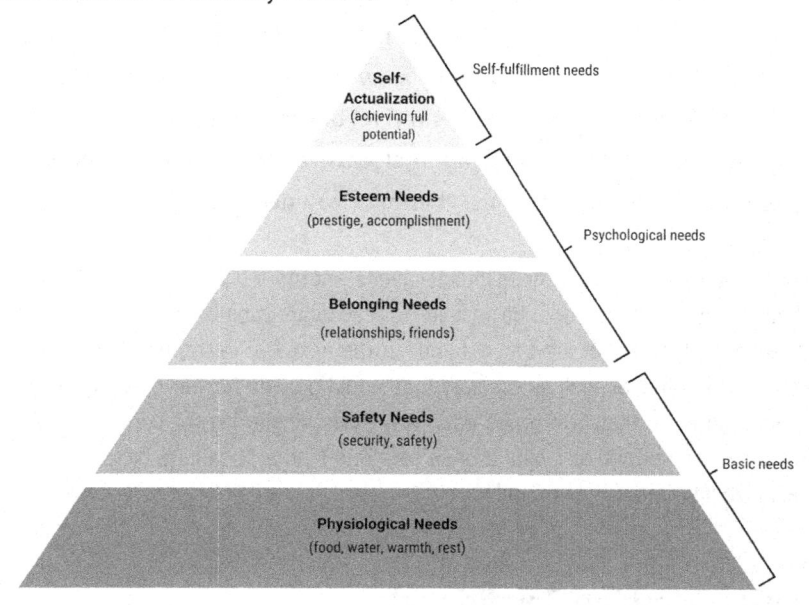

- **Self-Actualization** (achieving full potential) — Self-fulfillment needs
- **Esteem Needs** (prestige, accomplishment)
- **Belonging Needs** (relationships, friends) — Psychological needs
- **Safety Needs** (security, safety)
- **Physiological Needs** (food, water, warmth, rest) — Basic needs

With this viewpoint in mind, I encourage you to take this full-circle approach to your needs. Look at them holistically—as equal parts that live in harmony with one another rather than as building blocks (Figure 2-3).

Now that you understand this holistic view of human needs in general, let's apply them to your specific career needs.

Figure 2-3. A Full-Circle Approach to Needs

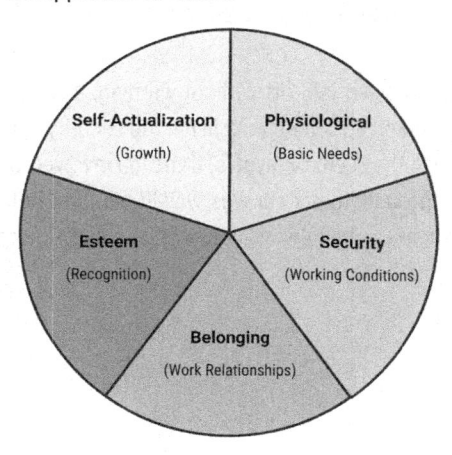

- Self-Actualization (Growth)
- Physiological (Basic Needs)
- Security (Working Conditions)
- Belonging (Work Relationships)
- Esteem (Recognition)

Physiological (Basic Needs)

When it comes to your career, there are basic needs that must be met to ensure you are physiologically comfortable at work; for example, a steady, stable income that allows you to not only survive, but live a high-quality life. Or you may require healthcare benefits, parental leave, or (for all the former educators out there) access to the restroom whenever you need it.

> When Brittany began to dive deep into her needs, she started thinking about what she specifically required, at the most basic level, to feel comfortable in the workplace. Because she was thinking about starting a family in the next few years, parental leave was at the top of her list, as well as a salary that would provide for her growing family. After commuting more than two hours each way every single day for her former employer, she decided to prioritize a hybrid or remote role with a 30-minute or less commute to maximize her time with her family.

Security (Working Conditions)

The physical and psychological conditions in which we work have a profound impact on our ability to do our jobs well. From a physical perspective, this can include specific safety equipment, reasonable accommodations for any disabilities, security systems, and the quality of the office location and furnishings. From a psychological viewpoint, examples include transparency in terms of job security and the organization's financial health, adequate paid time off (PTO) policies, insights into severance packages, and flexible scheduling.

> Because she'd previously been laid off without warning, it was especially important to Brittany that her next workplace offer clarity in her job security and what severance packages would be offered in the event of layoffs. If the job involved working in an office, she wanted to make sure the walk to her car was well-lit at night. Brittany's last role offered little to no flexibility in her schedule, so that was something else she was looking for going forward.

Belonging (Work Relationships)

We all want to feel a sense of belonging in life—that need is no different in our careers. This sense of belonging can manifest in our relationships with our team, supervisor, and peers, as well as organized internal communities, such as employee resource groups (ERGs). Also falling under "belonging" is the need to know how our work aligns with the organization's goals, as well as any organizational commitments to diversity, equity, and inclusion.

> In her previous position, Brittany never quite understood how her role and day-to-day work influenced the L&D department and the organization on a greater scale. After some reflection, she realized she wanted to clearly understand how her work fit into a bigger picture. While Brittany's basic needs led her to want a remote or hybrid role, she still wanted human connection. She decided to try work for an organization with company-sponsored events for everyone to meet and spend time together.

Esteem (Recognition)

According to a 2022 Gallup and Workhuman study, employees who receive the right amount of recognition for their work have lower burnout rates, improved daily emotions, and stronger relationships with their co-workers. Note, however, that everyone *receives* appreciation in the workplace differently—for some, it's as simple as being told "good job"; for others, this could look like getting to go home early on a Friday for a job well done. (I highly suggest reading *The Five Languages of Appreciation in the Workplace* by Gary Chapman.) Other examples include public recognition, peer-to-peer feedback, bonuses, and raises.

> As the first person to hold the curriculum designer role at her previous organization, Brittany often felt like no one quite knew what she did. As she assessed her needs in this category, she quickly realized that public recognition was important to her. She not only wants to know how she's contributing to the organization, she wants others to as well. As someone who also experiences imposter thinking, Brittany acknowledged that quick but frequent feedback and check-ins from her supervisor would help her recognize that she's on the right path.

Self-Actualization (Growth)

A study by Pew Research found that the number 1 reason people in the US left their jobs (67 percent) was due to "no opportunities for advancement" (Parker and Horowitz 2022). (Interestingly enough, this metric was tied with "pay was too low," which aligns with our other career need: physiological.) Career growth and advancement goals look different for everyone. For some, growth and advancement may mean the development of a new skill, or the opportunity to take on a new challenge. For others, this could look like the speed and prevalence of promotions and training opportunities, or the ability to mentor or be mentored. At its very core, a key to making sure your self-actualization need is met is ensuring you're given opportunities that allow you to succeed in your role.

> Having done L&D both formally and informally over the past few years, Brittany wanted to work for a company that could provide continuous, ongoing development. She'd attended talent development conferences and completed several certifications, but she was looking for long-term mentorship opportunities to continuously grow and evolve her craft. When she thought about her career growth, she knew her self-actualization would be fueled by having new opportunities to do challenging work that made a difference. She wasn't hungry to climb the corporate ladder; she simply wanted to find contentment and pride in her work.

A Full-Circle Approach in Action

Once you clearly define your career needs, you can begin identifying potential roles, organizations, leaders, and so on to meet these needs. Start by developing a list of "green flags"—clear definitions of what your needs look like in action—to use as a litmus test of whether an opportunity will meet your needs. In later chapters, we'll discuss how to do this while searching for roles, networking, and interviewing.

> As Brittany leaned more and more into her career needs, she began seeking out roles specifically aligned with them. She gained confidence to focus more on how the role would fill her needs during interviews rather than feeling like she had to prove herself.

Brittany applied to an L&D project manager role a few days after completing this assessment, and less than 24 hours later was selected for a first-round interview. The recruiter was so impressed with her confidence, clarity in what she wanted, and the value she brought that she was immediately moved on to the next round. After her interview, she sent me this message:

> "I just had the best interview experience ever! I asked him a lot of questions and he kept saying how impressed he was with my questions. I was able to speak confidently about what I'm currently doing, and the company culture sounds like it would be a great fit!"

Without knowing her career needs, Brittany would not have known what questions were most important to her. By taking the time to assess her needs, she was able to ensure that the roles she applied to were right for her. And, she could be confident that having her needs met would ultimately bring value to her role.

Activity

Now that you have been introduced to this new way of looking at Maslow's Hierarchy of Needs, use these self-reflection questions to assess yourself in each category.

Physiological needs:
- What are my essential financial and physical requirements for a comfortable work life?
- How do my health and energy levels influence my work? What do I need to maintain them?

Security needs:
- What factors contribute to my sense of job security and stability? How important are they to me?
- What measures or resources do I need to feel confident and secure in my career path?

Belonging needs:
- How important are workplace relationships to me? What kind of work environment helps me feel connected?
- What experiences have made me feel most part of a team? How can I seek more of them?

Esteem needs:
- What achievements or recognition do I need to feel valued and respected in my career?
- How do I define professional success? What steps can I take to enhance my self-esteem at work?

Self-actualization needs:
- What are my deepest passions and interests? How can I align them with my career goals?
- What personal and professional growth opportunities do I need to be fulfilled and reach my full potential?

Intentions Before Goals

How often do you focus on setting intentions *before* you set goals? It's one thing to set goals, but without intentions to lead them, most people lose momentum and start to question their capabilities. Now that you have clearly identified your career needs, it's time to set specific intentions to guide you as you develop your goals.

Setting intentions is not the same as blindly wishing for a million dollars to land in our laps—that's where most people go wrong. Rather than trying to "will" your goals into existence, setting an intention is about moving the needle in the direction you want to go.

The main difference between goals and intentions is the timeframe in which they work their magic. Intentions allow us to focus our energy on the present moment, while goals are focused on the future. Intentions answer the question "What am I going to embody now, even if I don't have it yet?" whereas goals answer the question "How am I going to make that a reality for myself?"

When setting intentions, you want them to be:
- **Aligned.** Your intentions should correspond with your needs, your why, and your L&D niche.
- **Specific.** Paint a clear picture of what you want to embody.
- **Present.** Write your intentions as if the outcome is already in existence.
- **Positive.** Your intentions should be heartfelt and come from a place of connection.

Here are a few examples of L&D career intentions:
- "I maintain a work-life balance."
- "I use my creative skills and talents."
- "I work with like-minded people where I feel supported."

> **Activity**
> Spend some time brainstorming aligned, specific, present, and positive career intentions.

As far as goals go, many people start with a big goal and then create small, micro-goals to help them accomplish the overarching goal. However, we're going to flip that on its head. Let's use our micro-goals to help us determine our overarching career goal.

When setting intention-led micro-goals, you want them to be:
- **Results-focused.** Identify the physical manifestation of your intentions.
- **Specific.** Be as exact, precise, and detailed as possible.
- **Short term.** Focus your micro-goal on the next step, not beyond.
- **Personal.** Align your micro-goal with what you want to do, not what you think you should do.

Here are a few micro-goals for the example L&D career intentions:
- "Schedule one to two 'me-time' activities each week."
- "Search for roles that allow me to be creative and reward me for my talents."
- "Find a community of like-minded L&D professionals to bounce ideas off of."

When you focus on creating intention-led micro-goals, you'll notice how many of them you can start achieving almost immediately. As you achieve each one, revisit your intention and set the next micro-goal, and then the next.

Setting your intentions and creating micro-goals isn't a "bunch of hocus pocus"—it's brain chemistry. A landmark study at the University of Texas concluded that visualization and intention setting is part of the process of setting and achieving goals, specifically because it is uniquely tied to emotional investment (Stuifbergen et al. 2003). When you visualize something and commit an intention to your long-term memory, it actually changes your brain structure.

In addition, your biochemistry also changes as you start achieving your micro-goals. This is because your body releases dopamine (the reward chemical) and serotonin (the happiness chvemical) when you achieve a goal, no matter how big or small (Fear 2022). That resulting feeling of satisfaction translates into motivation, which sets you up for success as you set and achieve your next micro-goal. Before you know it, you've used intention-led goals to rewire your brain, alter your biochemistry, and land your dream L&D role.

> **Activity**
> Develop one micro-goal per intention. Make sure it is results focused, specific, short term, and personal to you.

Setting REAL Goals

Now that we've started to set our intention-led micro-goals, it's time to identify the overarching goal for your next L&D career move. To do this, we are going to look at all your intentions and micro-goals and roll them up into one target REAL goal.

REAL vs. SMART Goals

SMART goals (specific, measurable, achievable, relevant, and time-bound) work for many situations, but there are too many variables when it comes to your L&D career for that formula to be effective. The biggest difference between a REAL goal and a SMART goal is what you have control over.

For example, while you may *want* to land a new role in 60 days, the reality is that there are too many variables and factors to include that timeframe in your goal. When our goals are too heavily influenced by external factors that are out of our control, we are more vulnerable to failure. Research shows that if we fail once at something (whether in our control or not), we are *more likely* to fail again at that goal. The more we focus on variables and factors outside our control, such as timeframe and measurability, the further away we may actually move from achieving our intended goal.

I suggest creating REAL goals instead:
- **Realistic**. Focus on what is mostly in your control, as well as what's practical and reasonable for your next career move.
- **Energizing**. Create a goal that is motivating. Not only will you be energized once you achieve it, but the mere thought of working toward it energizes you.
- **Aligned**. Use your needs, intentions, and micro-goals to create your overarching goal.
- **Latent**. Keep your goals to yourself. Peter Gollwitzer (2009) and his colleagues found that the simple act of sharing a goal publicly can make you less likely to achieve it. His research found that telling people what you want to achieve can create a premature sense of completeness, which may initially leave you with a sense of pride, but may ultimately (and quickly) lead to a loss of motivation.

Meet Meghan: As a seasoned L&D leader, Meghan was looking for her next big role in the talent development space. Before we started working together, Meghan had created this SMART goal:

"Within three months, land a talent development role using my skills in coaching, cultural program design, problem solving, and relationship building."

While this SMART goal was a good start, it was focused on the time-bound variable that was out of her control. We also realized that, while it was fairly realistic, her goal was missing pieces that made it energizing and aligned. With REAL goals in mind, Meghan changed her focus to a new goal:

"Take my leadership capabilities to the next level as an L&D department leader in a role that relies on my program design, coaching, relationship, and problem-solving skills, and work for an organization and team that promotes consistent feedback, collaboration, and flexible scheduling."

In her current position, Meghan was already an L&D leader with a small team under her. Thus, her REAL goal was realistic and, more importantly, did not focus on anything that was out of her control. Each part represented something she could actively search for. Additionally, Meghan energized her goal by adding details about what would excite her most in her next role—taking her leadership capabilities to the next level. While her SMART goal highlighted skills she wanted to use, Meghan's REAL goal expanded on them by aligning with her needs, intentions, and micro-goals. After settling on this REAL goal, Meghan shared it with no one (other than me) and reflected on it daily.

> **Activity**
> Have you already set an overarching career goal for yourself? Is it a REAL goal? If not, how can you make it more realistic, energizing, and aligned? Once you've identified your REAL goal, write it down, keep it to yourself, and reflect on it daily.

Timelines vs. Timeframes

When you think about your next L&D career goal, do you already have a timeframe in mind for achieving it? If so, that's a natural thought. While most goals (especially in a corporate environment) require a timeframe to help ensure they are accomplished, career goals require you to look at time from a different lens.

As we discovered in the SMART versus REAL goal setting section, time-bound career goals tie us to a time standard that is out of our control. You have no influence over when roles are posted, the speed of the hiring process, or what roles you'll be offered—the more you focus on time in your career goals, the more likely you'll end up feeling defeated if that day comes and goes.

Rather than setting a *timeframe*, which is rigid and has a definitive end date, I recommend creating a *timeline*. Your timeline should be firm enough to provide accountability and structure, but flexible enough to shift to accommodate external factors outside your control.

This is not to say you can't have an end date in mind. However, instead of starting with that date and reverse engineering into it, start by considering the following factors:

- **Urgency.** *How quickly do you need to get out of your current role or into a new role?* There may be more urgency if you're recently

unemployed or in a toxic work environment, or less urgency if you are really happy in your role and just starting to consider what is next for you.
- **Time**. *How much time can you dedicate to your search?* While a job search or career transition should never become a full-time role, the amount of time you can dedicate to it will ultimately influence how long the process takes. If you can only dedicate 15-minutes a week, it's unlikely that you'll be able to find and land a role in 30 days.
- **Preparedness**. *Do you need to upskill in anything? Is your resume up to date?* Do you have a network you can leverage? Laying the groundwork to find a new role requires preparation. The amount of preparation you need and want to do will influence when you're ready to start applying and interviewing for new L&D roles.

The key is to take your level of urgency, time, and preparedness into consideration as you determine your job search timeline. This can help you define a working or tentative end date, rather than arbitrarily choosing a specific date that may, or may not, be in your control.

In chapter 1, we looked at the four L&D career success codes—the ABCDs. Using those as a framework—combined with your tentative end date based on the reality of your urgency, time, and preparedness—you can now create a flexible timeline.

Let's review a few sample timelines.

High Urgency, High Time, Low Preparedness

For a recently laid off client of mine, time was of the essence. He was unemployed, which meant he had a lot of time to dedicate to his L&D job search, but he wasn't prepared to be job searching (very low preparedness). His timeline initially focused heavily on finding alignment and then quickly moved into areas of development (Figure 2-4). Because his time was "high" (meaning he had a lot of it to use), he could work on multiple success codes at the same time.

Figure 2-4. High Urgency, High Time, Low Preparedness Timeline

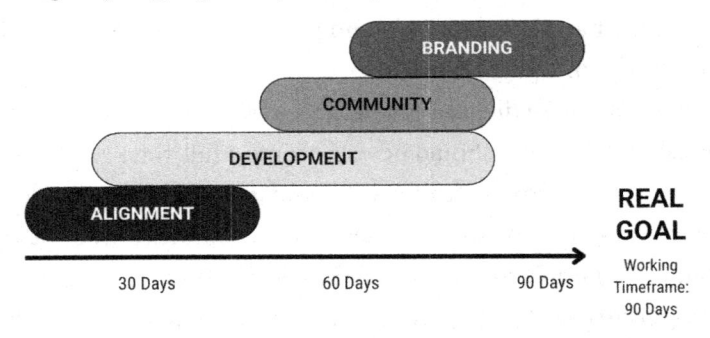

```
                                    BRANDING
                            COMMUNITY
                    DEVELOPMENT
            ALIGNMENT                                   REAL
                                                        GOAL
                                                        Working
         30 Days        60 Days         90 Days         Timeframe:
                                                        90 Days
```

Low Urgency, Low Time, Low Preparedness

This client came to me in the early stages of her career transition from higher education to the corporate L&D world. She was very happy in her role at a university but knew she was ready to make a change. While she did not have a lot of urgency (she wanted to make a change in about a year), being a single mom and working full time meant she didn't have much spare time for focusing on a career change. On top of that, because this was her first corporate L&D role, she needed to focus on her development before beginning the application process. Her limited time meant that she needed to avoid overlapping success codes as much as possible (Figure 2-5).

Figure 2-5. Low Urgency, Low Time, Low Preparedness Timeline

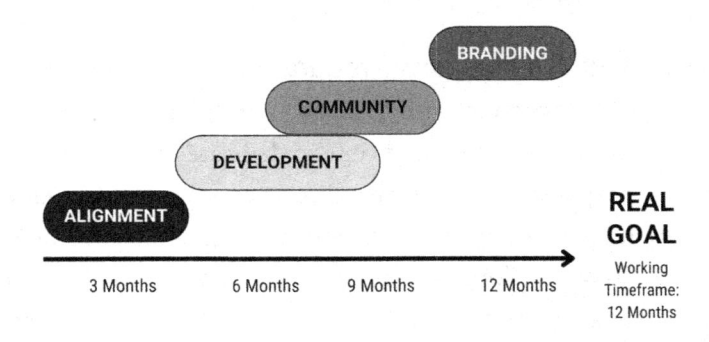

```
                                            BRANDING
                                COMMUNITY
                    DEVELOPMENT
        ALIGNMENT                                       REAL
                                                        GOAL
                                                        Working
        3 Months    6 Months    9 Months   12 Months    Timeframe:
                                                        12 Months
```

Medium Urgency, Medium Time, High Preparedness

When this client and I began working together, they had already been actively searching for a few months and had spent a significant amount of time preparing for their new role. Currently a senior instructional designer, they wanted a role that was more focused on project and program management, and had recently obtained a certification in project management. With their preparedness high, this client decided to immediately focus on overlapping alignment and branding, to present themselves as a subject matter expert (SME) in project and program management (Figure 2-6). The rest of their timeline was dedicated to creating community.

Figure 2-6. Medium Urgency, Medium Time, High Preparedness Timeline

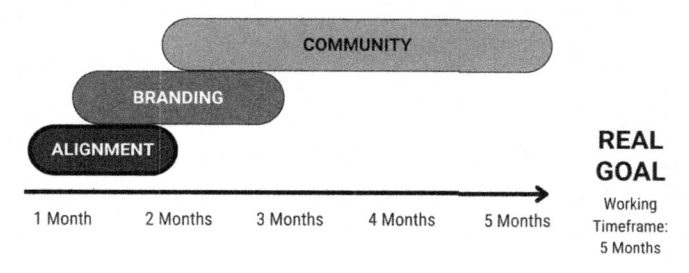

Remember, the purpose of a timeline is to provide flexibility in your approach to reaching your REAL goal. Your timeline will continuously ebb and flow based on variables both inside and outside your control.

> **Activity**
> When you think about landing your next L&D role, do you have a timeframe in mind? Rather than focusing on a timeframe, take a few minutes to consider your urgency, time, and preparedness and build out a timeline.

What's Next? Putting Your REAL Goals Into Action

You've done a lot of career soul searching in this chapter, so here's a few ways to make sure you put that work into action:

- Check in with your intentions and micro-goals daily. The more you can actively catch yourself reaching your goals, the more motivated you'll be to continue on.

- Review your REAL goal and create a timeline that aligns with your urgency, availability, and preparedness. Be honest with yourself about the reality of all three and remember that you're creating a fluid timeline, not a rigid timeframe.
- It's OK to be overwhelmed by your goal (even if it energizes you)—in the next chapter, we'll focus on how to start building the confidence you need to make your REAL goal your real life.

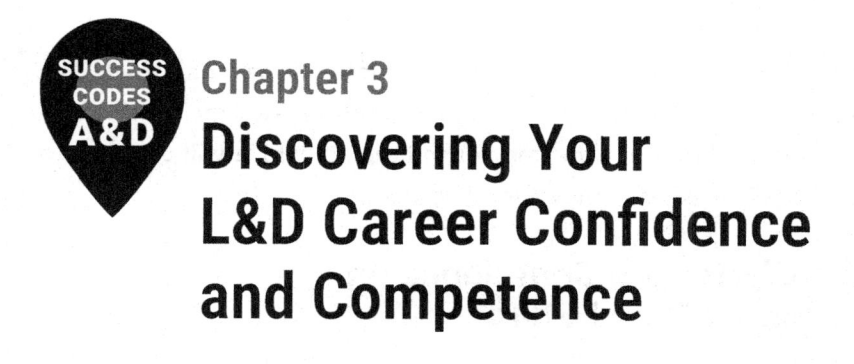

# Chapter 3
Discovering Your L&D Career Confidence and Competence

"With confidence you have won even before you have started."
—Marcus Garvey

Think about *one word* that describes how you currently feel about making a career change in the TD field. What comes to mind?

In a recent poll I conducted with more than 200 jobseekers, 52 percent said *uncertain* or *unsure* was the first word that came to mind when describing how they felt about their job search, followed by 30 percent who said they felt *demoralized*.

Here's an eye-opening fact: A 2016 research study looking at the correlation between uncertainty and confidence found that "confidence is a form of certainty" (Pouget, Drugowitsch, and Kepecs 2016). So, if you feel unsure or uncertain about your next career move, there is a high probability that your uncertainty will manifest as a lack of confidence. If you're not confident in your next move, you'll continue to feel uncertain—and the cycle will continue.

So where do you start when it comes to breaking this cycle? According to Alyssa Dver, founder of the American Confidence Institute and author of *Confidence Is a Choice*, you first have to operate on this principle: Confidence is being *certain enough* about the truth of something.

Once you've established that principle, you can then begin building enough certainty through gaining clarity. You'll explore the factual evidence of your past and use what you learn to gain clarity about the vision of your future, your strengths, and the path you are choosing to take in your TD career. When you are certain enough of your future vision, and the skills and abilities needed to get there, that certainty manifests itself as confidence. The more confidence you have in your vision, skills, and abilities, the easier it is to feel more certain about the direction you're heading, which will continue to manifest as confidence—and the cycle will repeat.

Getting Clarity and Confidence on the Vision for Your Future

Before you start thinking about the future, you need to hop back into the past to suss out any root source thoughts that are influencing your ability to objectively see your future. I like to imagine that these root-source thoughts—our natural, conscious thoughts about ourselves—can easily fog our vision like a pair of glasses exposed to a quick change in temperature. When the vision of your future is fogged, it's easy to feel uncertain, which can cause you to quickly fall back into that lack of certainty–lack of confidence cycle.

> **Activity**
> Let's start by assessing your root source thinking. Take three to five minutes and write down as many thoughts about yourself as you can—good, bad, or indifferent, write them all down. Once you have a list of root source thoughts, circle the ones you believe may be or are getting in the way of your L&D career success.

Once you have uncovered some of your more limiting root source thoughts, you can start to understand how they fog your vision, influence your behavior, and continue the cycle (Figure 3-1).

Additionally, root source thoughts can quickly turn into internal beliefs. Your internal self-beliefs are what you hold to be true about you—whether they factually are true or not. These self-beliefs, in turn, influence your internal dialogue—that subconscious voice in your head commenting on your situation. This is where we start to see the internal conversation stemming from what we hold to be true about ourselves.

As adults gain new experiences, our brains change through a process called *synaptic pruning*, in which some synapse connections are strengthened while

Figure 3-1. The Root Source Thought Cycle

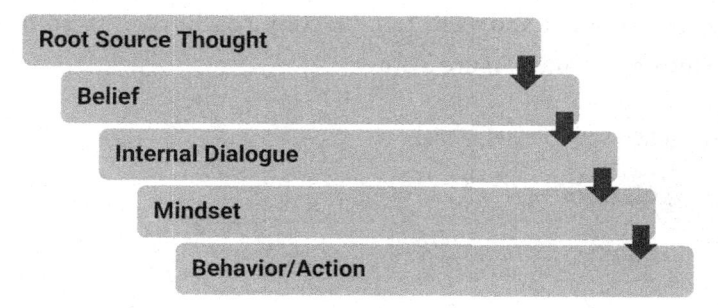

- Root Source Thought
- Belief
- Internal Dialogue
- Mindset
- Behavior/Action

others are eliminated. The more we train our brain through our own internal dialogue, the stronger those synapses become and the tighter we hold those root source thoughts as truths. This, in turn, has the power to shift our mindset about the situation we are currently in.

When your mind has been made up, and your mindset fixed on a specific outcome or feeling, you begin to exhibit behaviors and actions aligned with that mindset. According to Jodie Lowinger (2023), "Your mindset will dictate the actions you take to achieve and sustain success as well as how you go about problem solving and generating ideas. Not only does your mindset guide your actions, it guides how you react too."

> **Meet Caroline:** When I first met Caroline, she held this root source thought to be true: "No one will ever want to hire a professor for an L&D role." This led her to the self-belief that she would never be good enough to land the type of L&D role she actually wanted. The more Caroline leaned into that belief, the more her inner dialogue rallied around it, reminding her of past failures, rejections from roles she really wanted, and the quickly approaching date she'd set for herself to enter a new role. As this inner dialogue continued to remind Caroline of all the ways her L&D career search wasn't working for her, it began to shift her mindset into one of desperation, and she consistently felt unsure of herself and started to doubt the skills and abilities she worked so hard to obtain.
>
> Caroline began to panic that her L&D career goals were never going to come true and she started to abandon her job search completely. She stopped networking with peers and began only applying to roles she was outrageously overqualified for, in hopes something would bite. Nothing did, and these actions and behaviors (or lack thereof) only deepened Caroline's root source thoughts, perpetuating the cycle.

So, how did Caroline turn it around and land her dream L&D role as an educational consultant and executive function coach? She began by starting with the future in mind (Figure 3-2).

Figure 3-2. Action-Led Mindset Model

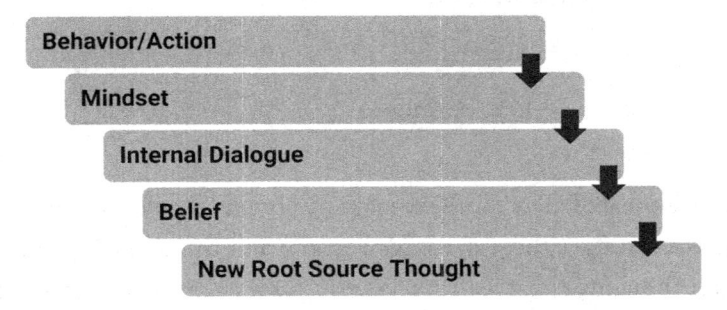

- Behavior/Action
- Mindset
- Internal Dialogue
- Belief
- New Root Source Thought

> **Activity**
> Before we flip the root source thinking model on its head, follow this prompt and take a few minutes to visualize and write down your thoughts.
>
> Imagine you are waking up one year from now, and you've landed your dream L&D role. What does a "day in the life" look like for you? How do you feel throughout the day? How do you feel at the end of the day? What words would you use to describe your life? What behaviors and actions did this future version of you do to get to live this life and have this career?

Let's start with behaviors and actions. In psychology, "'Act As If' is a behavioral strategy that encourages individuals to consciously adopt the mindset and behaviors of the person they aspire to become" (CBT Los Angeles 2023). This lived experience begins to retrain the brain. By consistently engaging in the behaviors associated with your L&D career goals, you can alter your self-perception and mindset. As your mindset changes, your internal dialogue shifts to match that new state of being, which ultimately reinforces your positive self-beliefs. The more you believe positively in yourself, the more you can capitalize on the root source thoughts that are serving you and recognize (and often diminish) the root source thoughts that are not.

Enough was enough—Caroline decided not to let her desperation win. She inventoried the behaviors and actions that someone who reached her L&D career goals would focus on and set out to embody them daily. For Caroline, this included creating and sharing content on LinkedIn, ramping up her networking, and maintaining a strong personal brand. The more she focused on these actions, the more her mindset began to shift. Because she believed she was creating content that was aligned with her strengths, she couldn't wait to put it out into the world. Her internal dialogue also changed—rather than constantly reminding her of her failures, it started to more quickly notice her small wins. The more that inner dialogue focused on her microachievements (whether a comment on a post she created or a great networking conversation), the more her beliefs started to shift.

For the first time in a long time, Caroline began to feel hopeful that her skills would be appreciated by the right company for the right role. This conscious thought activity effectively eliminated her root source thought that no one would ever want to hire a professor for an L&D role.

I knew the day Caroline's confidence rose to the top when I received a short, yet powerful message from her that said: "I just took a look at my resume again, and WOW, I'd totally hire me." She no longer needed external validation to create her confidence—it 100 percent came from within. Less than 30 days later, Caroline was offered her dream L&D role.

What I hope you take from Caroline's story, and others like it, is that confidence is a choice, and confident people consciously decide to be confident. It didn't happen overnight for Caroline, but by consciously deciding to rewrite her confidence narrative and clarifying a future vision for herself, she took control of her root source thoughts so they could no longer control her.

"Confidence is a conscious, controllable thought—in fact, it's a thought about another thought that scientists call metacognition," says Alyssa Dver (n.d.). "You don't feel confident or become confident. You decide if you are confident about something."

Gaining Clarity (and Confidence) in Your Abilities

When your confidence begins to waver, you may begin to doubt your own abilities and diminish your skill set. This can lead you down a slippery spiral: the vicious application cycle (Figure 3-3).

Figure 3-3. The Vicious Application Cycle

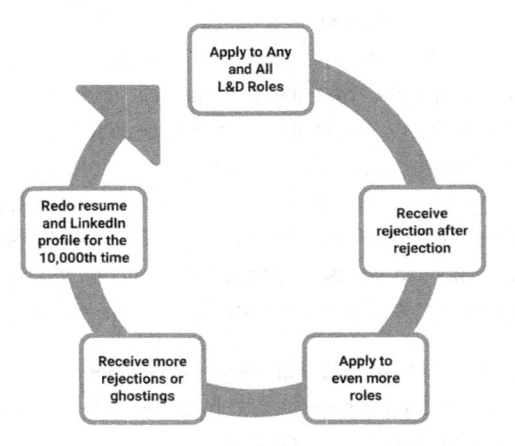

```
         Apply to Any
         and All
         L&D Roles
    ↗                  ↘
Redo resume              Receive
and LinkedIn             rejection after
profile for the          rejection
10,000th time
    ↖                  ↙
Receive more         Apply to
rejections or        even more
ghostings            roles
```

The vicious application cycle occurs when you lack clarity about your skills and values. The more "foggy" you are about what you bring to the table, the harder it becomes to imagine what the right role actually looks like.

If you're not sure how your skills, interests, and values will translate into your next L&D career move, you may be tempted to cast a wide net and apply to any and all L&D roles you see. While many people abide by the outdated advice of "the more you apply, the more interviews you'll receive"—the truth couldn't be further from that. In fact, the more you apply to arbitrary jobs and the wider a net you cast, the more rejections you'll receive. As the rejections pile on, you'll inevitably get the urge to completely abandon your current resume or CV, cover letter, portfolio, and so on, to start from scratch.

By casting such a wide net, you've robbed yourself of any evidence to support whether your resume (or any of your other marketing or branding materials) is working. Rather than pausing, most people double down and continue the "throw spaghetti at the wall" approach in the hope that something will stick. Inevitably, this leads to more rejections, which may lead many people to redo their marketing and branding materials yet again. And the cycle continues.

Does this sound familiar? Maybe you're in this cycle or have been in the past. Or maybe you know someone deep in its trenches. The good news is that there is not only a way out of the cycle, but also a way to avoid it altogether.

Using the L&D Career Clarity Funnel, you'll start with reconnecting with your values, skills, and strengths and end by identifying any immediate gaps (Figure 3-4). When you are clear on what you already have, it makes what you need to improve on seem a lot less daunting and, perhaps, even exciting.

Figure 3-4. The L&D Career Clarity Funnel

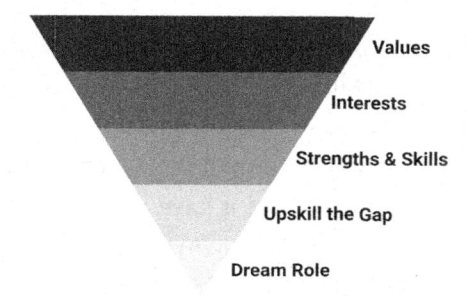

- Values
- Interests
- Strengths & Skills
- Upskill the Gap
- Dream Role

Core Values

Let's start by taking a high-level look at your core values. Further chapters will dive deeper into understanding and dissecting your core values as they relate to your ideal company, but for now we are looking at them internally—they're your secret confidence weapon. When you can clearly pinpoint your personal core values, it aids you in three specific ways:

- **Decision making.** Knowing your core values allows you to make decisions faster and more decisively, because you can quickly align with decisions that are most important to you.
- **Self-image.** Values are a core part of how we see ourselves. By knowing your values, you're able to gain clarity about what you stand for and build beliefs and habits in support of your values.
- **Behaviors.** We are all subject to social and societal pressures—some support us, while others can be perceived as destructive. When your values are clear, it's easier to seek out people who are aligned with your values and amplify your positive behaviors. Alternatively, it provides a window into people and behaviors that have a negative influence on you.

> **Activity**
> Take a few moments to reflect on your core values. Write down the top three to five that come to mind. How have they served you in terms of your decision making, self-image, and behaviors?

Interests

Before we explore your key skills, let's look at your interests. We'll focus first on interests because L&D professionals have a tendency to latch on to skills they've had success with, even if they've outgrown them. For example, I cultivated and excelled at the skill of facilitation and it gave me energy to use that skill for many years—until it didn't. While I recognized that I was getting burned out and had outgrown facilitating, I kept taking on facilitation opportunities and kept burning out. My confidence began to suffer. I thought, "Has the one skill I leaned on my entire L&D career failed me? What else am I good for?"

This was when I learned the importance of identifying future career interests before lasering in on my current career skill set. While your future career interests may be expanded versions of your current skills, it's also important to reflect on newer interests that you want to become skills.

> **Activity**
> Earlier in this chapter, you visualized an ideal day in your new L&D role one year from now. It's time to revisit that vision.
>
> > Take a few moments to reflect. What interests are you pursuing in your career a year from now? What are you doing at work that energizes you? Write down three to five career interests you'd like to explore more in your next L&D role.

Skills

Now, let's explore your current L&D skills. Over the course of your entire career—regardless of where you are currently in your journey—you've picked up a collection of specific skills. What is so special about learning and talent development is that no skills are specifically unique to this field. L&D is made up of transferable skills from many industries, including marketing, education, and technology.

What does this mean for you? Your skills, whether developed directly in the L&D field or not, are fair game when it comes to your L&D career move.

> **Activity**
>
> Let's revisit your ideal day visualization one more time.
>
> Take a few moments to reflect on your vision. What skills are you leveraging in your new role that you developed over the course of your career? What strengths will you lean on to be successful in this role? What skills are you ready to leave behind as you begin this new role? Write down three to five career skills you'd like to bring with you to your next L&D role.

Upskill the Gap

Now that you have a combined list of six to 10 career interests and skills that you envision taking with you to your next L&D role, let's perform a mini skills and interest confidence gap assessment (Table 3-1). As L&D pros, we know how important gap assessments are for gaining certainty (and in return confidence) that our learning programs are going to work. The same thing goes for your own skills and interest assessment. In later chapters, we'll dive into how to create a professional development plan for your areas of opportunity, but right now we'll focus on how the assessment piece can increase your certainty and confidence.

First, you need to establish a baseline (your current state) and your envisioned future state (where you want to be next in your L&D career). This involves doing a skills and interest gap assessment (Table 3-1).

Once you've completed the assessment, you can be certain enough of your current skill sets and interests, as well as how they will serve you in your next role. Whether they are skills you're building competence in (anything rated a 1 or 2), skills you're expanding your knowledge of (anything marked a 3), or skills you know like the back of your hand (4 and 5), you can now confidently identify how you're going to bring your future career vision to life.

> **Activity**
>
> Think about how you are currently using each of the skills and interests you identified in the previous activities in this chapter (or maybe how you've used them in the past). What does it look like to put that skill into practice or action? (Note: If it is a new interest, consider what you've been doing to explore that interest, or how it was piqued.) Create a gap assessment like the sample in Table 3-1 and record each skill and interest.
>
> After you've defined how you're currently using each skill and interest, use this scale to rate your competence level. Record your answers in the table.
>
> - **5: Expert level.** This skill is second nature. You excel at all aspects and can easily teach and lead others in this area.
> - **4: Very comfortable.** You are proficient. You can tackle advanced tasks with confidence and may provide guidance to others.
> - **3: Enough working knowledge.** You can independently handle standard tasks. You understand key aspects but may not be adept at more complex challenges.
> - **2: Developing competence.** You have a basic grasp of the skill and can perform simple tasks with guidance. You're still learning the fundamentals but are no longer a complete beginner.
> - **1: Still a beginner.** You're just starting out. You're learning the basics and need significant guidance.
>
> Once you've identified how you're using your skills and interests, begin to consider how you want to use them in your next role. This is your first opportunity to begin defining your next role on your own terms.
>
> Now, rate your desired future competence levels for each skill or interest and record them in the table. (Note: In some instances, how you're currently using your skills and interests is also how you want to use them in your next role. If that's true for you, note that too.)

Table 3-1. Example Skills and Interest Gap Assessment

Name	Is It a Skill or an Interest?	How Are You Currently Using It?	Competence in Current State	How Do You Want to Use It?	Competence in Future State
Project management	Skill	Overseeing project and program timelines, due dates, communications, and reporting	4	Same	4
Curriculum design	Skill	Designing specific learning assets for entire learning programs and curriculums	5	Oversee the curriculum design strategy, in addition to designing learning assets	5
Communications and marketing	Interest	Learning more about using marketing techniques while rolling out L&D programs	3	Own all external communications from L&D department to organization for new and existing learning programs	4
Coaching	Interest	Mentoring new team members	1	Provide more formalized coaching sessions to new and existing team members on career and skill development	2
Data analysis	Skill	Pulling and synthesizing data and metrics for select learning programs	4	Own the data analysis for all programming and the recommendations process based off the data	3
Facilitation	Skill	Leading all new hire instructor-led training and virtual instructor-led training learning experiences	5	Lead all leadership instructor-led training and virtual instructor-led training learning experiences	5
Leadership development	Interest	Reviewing needs assessments for department heads and providing recommendations for leadership development programming	2	Actively consult with department heads on leadership development needs and create an internal leadership development strategy	3.5

Discovering Your L&D Career Confidence and Competence

> **Talent Development Career Pathways Tool**
> If you need some inspiration in terms of the types of skills you see more often in the L&D field, ATD has a career pathway tool that outlines different skill sets and where they fall in terms of different L&D job families. Learn more at td.org/career-pathways.

Creating Your Own Personal Development Plan

L&D practitioners are both blessed and cursed with our quest for knowledge and development—it's in our bones and it's why we do what we do. That quest can lead us down the road of endless courses, certifications, programs, and even degrees, but it might not get us any closer to our next dream role.

There is no one-size-fits all solution to developing skills. And yet when we turn the attention to ourselves, I find that many job-seeking L&D folks are quick to seek out an upskilling silver bullet that will make them more marketable. Don't fall into that trap. Instead, you need to create your own personal development plan (PDP).

Self-Development Mindset Shift

The first word in self-development is *self*—meaning whatever you choose to upskill in, it has to come from an *internal desire* to grow in that skill set. I've worked with countless clients over the years who placed a higher value on a "more marketable" course, program, or certification, only to realize after investing time, money, and resources that it was not a skill they desired to use, and in fact, drained their energy.

When crafting a PDP, ask yourself, "What do I want to grow my area of expertise in?" Don't focus on what you think others want to see from you.

Putting Your PDP Together

Once you have a clearer understanding of your competencies, you can begin to focus on building a *unique* personal development plan. I promise it's much easier (and cheaper) than you think.

Rather than focusing on a one-size-fits-all program or certification, refer to your lists of skills and interests and start with the ones that have the biggest competence gap. For example, in Table 3-1, the leadership development skill had one of the biggest deltas (1.5).

Once you've identified the biggest gaps, focus on how you want to use this skill in the future and begin sourcing your own learning content. To improve the leadership development skill from Table 3-1, you would want to search for learning resources on consulting with department heads (which could include communication best practices), as well as tools or models for leadership development. Remember, personal development isn't just about completing a course, so make sure you're also adding resources to your PDP, such as books, online resources (such as blogs and tool kits), conferences, podcasts, certifications, and memberships and communities.

> **AI Pro Tip**
>
> Rather than scouring the internet for endless opportunities to upskill, let a generative AI tool like ChatGPT or Perplexity help you! Upload a copy of your skills and interests gap assessment and use a prompt like this one:
>
> Act as an expert in putting together aligned and modern personal development plans for learning and development practitioners, who are searching for their next role in the field. [*You can even get creative here and add more context about the type of role you're looking for.*] Attached you will find a skills gap assessment, in which the L&D practitioner named and described the current use of each skill and interest, as well as how they would like to upskill in this particular skill set.
>
> Based on this personal development skills gap assessment, put together a specific personal development plan for this L&D practitioner, along with the resources to develop each skill. This plan can include coursework, programs, certifications, events, online toolkits, blog articles, podcasts, conferences, memberships, associations, webinars, YouTube videos, and so on.
>
> Please map out the personal development plan over the course of [*insert your timeframe*], starting with the skills and interests with the biggest competency gap.
>
> You'll be amazed at how quickly you'll have a customized PDP at your fingertips!

At the end of the day, competence equals confidence. The more confident you are in your skills, the deeper you'll be able to go in your competencies—it's a never-ending process that continues to fuel itself—once you hyper-focus on the right development areas.

What's Next? Putting Your Clarity and Confidence Into Practice

Now that you have gained clarity and become certain enough about your vision of the future, as well as the skills, interests, and abilities you will use to make that a reality, it's time to put it all into practice.

- Put your L&D career vision into writing and place it somewhere you'll see it daily. The more you immerse yourself in the vision of your career future, the more likely you'll find proof you're moving in the right direction. The more proof your brain finds, the more certain you'll become, and the more certain you become, the more confidence you'll gain.
- Focus on building your competence in any of the areas you marked as a one or two in your gap assessment. This allows you to start developing for the parts versus the whole, which can feel overwhelming and uncertain. Focusing only on areas where you need to build competence will increase your certainty in that skill set.
- As you go through the next few chapters, you may find that the skills and interests you highlighted in this chapter shift—that's totally normal! Just make sure to adjust your PDP to reflect any changes.

Chapter 4
Finding Your L&D Niche

SUCCESS CODE A

"To live is to choose. But to choose well, you must know who you are and what you stand for, where you want to go and why you want to get there." —Kofi Annan

If you're looking to grow and evolve in your L&D career, most L&D career advice will tell you to start by choosing a title you're interested in, searching for jobs based on that title, and creating a resume tailored to each job description.

The problem with this one-size-fits-all approach is that it automatically assumes all roles are created equal when it comes to job title, and it leaves out a key component—you.

Just as we know there's no such thing as effective one-size-fits-all learning, the same is true when it comes to growing your L&D career. Your plan needs to be tailored specifically to you.

This is where determining your L&D niche comes in.

What Is an L&D Niche?

When people first hear the term *L&D niche*, they automatically assume it means picking a job title that best suits what they want to do next (such as senior instructional designer, L&D program manager, or chief learning officer). But when we try to squeeze into the box of a specific job title, we limit our opportunities.

Your L&D niche is the intersection between your skills, your interests, and your values (which you started uncovering in chapter 3). At its simplest, it explains, in one sentence, what you do, how you do it, and whom you want to do it for. Rather than trying to fit into every job description you think you should be applying to, your L&D niche allows you to create your own box and find roles that are aligned with what you want to do next, regardless of specific job titles.

In essence, your L&D niche is your career North Star, providing a new and aligned approach to actually finding and landing your dream L&D role.

How to Find Your L&D Niche

Figure 4-1. The Three Parts of Your L&D Niche

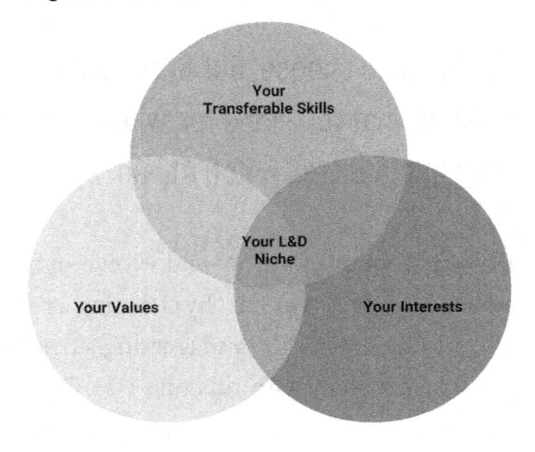

Your L&D niche has three main parts (Figure 4-1):

- The transferable skills you've gained in your experience thus far
- The interests that you want to explore in your next role
- The values you have and want to share with your next organization

When you identify all three parts, you can begin to clearly articulate what you want to do next, how you want to do it, and what type of organization or team you'd like to do it for.

To find your L&D niche, follow these steps:

1. Determine your legacy (your why).
2. Articulate your next step (your impact).
3. Identify your skills and interests (your how).
4. Define your core values (your who).

Step 1. Determine Your Legacy (Your Why)

No matter where you are on your L&D career journey, it's important to kick off finding your niche with the end in mind. Similar to creating meaningful and effective learning experiences, our end goals must be at the forefront to make sure we are creating learning content that's aligned with expected outcomes.

Take a few moments to imagine your retirement party. Everyone you've ever cared for, worked with, and created learning for is in attendance to see you off into retirement. Each person comes up and thanks you for what you've achieved and the impact you've had—what are they saying to you? What do you ultimately want to be remembered for? Here's an example: *"I want to be remembered for creating welcoming experiences that engage, inspire, and enlighten."*

When you synthesize your legacy, you create a target to shoot your L&D career arrow toward. In other words, you have your why.

> **Activity**
>
> When you retire from your long, fruitful L&D career, what do you want to be remembered for? Once you have your legacy, you can capture it in your L&D Career Golden Circle, which I've adapted from Simon Sinek's Golden Circle (Figure 4-2). (Sinek's circle starts with why in the innermost circle, then how as the middle circle, and what as the outermost circle.)
>
> **Figure 4-2.** Your L&D Career Golden Circle
>
> Concentric circles labeled from outside in: What, Who (values), How, Impact, Why.

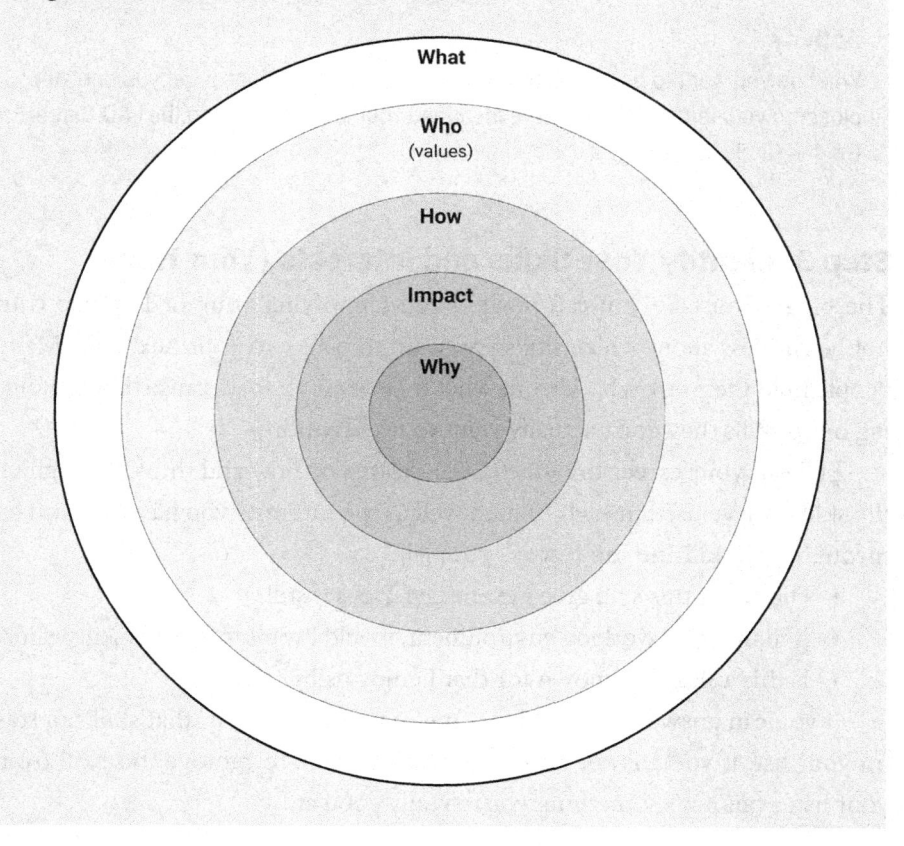

Step 2. Articulate Your Next Step (Your Impact)

Once you can tap into your legacy, you can start thinking about how to get there. How does your next career move get you one step closer to achieving that legacy?

Start brainstorming what you want to be known for in your next role. I call this "the office walk-by test." Imagine you are in your next, dreamy L&D role, sitting in a bright office (even if you want to work remotely, just go with me for this one). Two co-workers pass by the door. One of them turns to the other, points to your office, and says, "Who's that?" The other co-worker immediately says, "Oh, that's [*insert your name here*], they [*what you are known for*]. For example: "Oh, that's Emma. She develops and leads our next-level onboarding programs!"

> **Activity**
> What do you want to be known for in your next role? How does it get you one step closer to your legacy? Once you've identified your impact, add it to the L&D Career Golden Circle in Figure 4-2.

Step 3. Identify Your Skills and Interests (Your How)

The biggest mistake you can make when identifying your L&D niche is to not be ruthless about which skills you want to take into your next role. Many people hold themselves back from what they want to do, because they're holding on to skills they don't actually want to use anymore.

Pull out your career timeline (L&D-related or not) and think through all the skills you've used in each role, as well as the interests you have. As you go through each skill and interest ask yourself:

- Did using this skill give me energy? Does it still?
- If in the right working environment, would I want to use this skill again?
- Is this a skill I'm known for that I enjoy using?

If you can answer yes to at least one of those questions, that skill can stay on your list. If you answer no to all three, it's time to remove this skill from your list, even if it's something you're really good at.

Here is an example: *"I design and deliver next-level onboarding programs by leveraging coaching, facilitation, and program design and management skills for organizations that value innovation, autonomy, and sustainability."* Within this niche statement, you can find dozens of titles that align with what you want to do, how you want to do it, and who you want to do it for.

Step 5. Identify the Right Roles

Having an L&D niche gives you the freedom to operate beyond specific job titles; however, it's important to have a general understanding of the types of roles you can expect to find in your niche.

To start exploring roles aligned with your skills, interests, and values, you'll want to use a job search engine like LinkedIn Jobs or Indeed to conduct a Boolean search, which allows you to combine keywords from the "how" of your L&D Career Golden Circle with operators (such as AND, OR, and NOT) to include or exclude certain terms from the results. This type of search makes it easier to find roles that align with your specific L&D career interests.

Here are a few rules of thumb for conducting a Boolean search:

- Always include "Learning" in your Boolean search.
- The operators (AND, OR, and NOT) typically need to be in all caps.
- Follow the 3 x 5 rule. You should aim for three to five sets of search terms, inclusive of three to five words each. For example:
    - Learning AND Coaching AND Program Design AND Onboarding
    - Learning AND Onboarding AND Program Management AND Leadership
    - Learning AND Leadership OR Executive AND Facilitation
    - Learning AND Analysis AND Onboarding AND Program Management
    - Learning AND Employee Experience AND Onboarding AND Facilitation
    - Learning AND Instructional Design OR Curriculum Development NOT Facilitation

Activity

Once you've played around with your Boolean search, start adding roles that align to your L&D Career Golden Circle in Figure 4-2. (Note that it may take a few days for the search engine algorithm to catch on to your search pattern, especially if you've been searching for roles solely based on job title.)

Figure 4-3 presents a completed L&D Career Golden Circle, which takes the example we've gone through from Steps 1 to 5.

Figure 4-3. An Example L&D Career Golden Circle

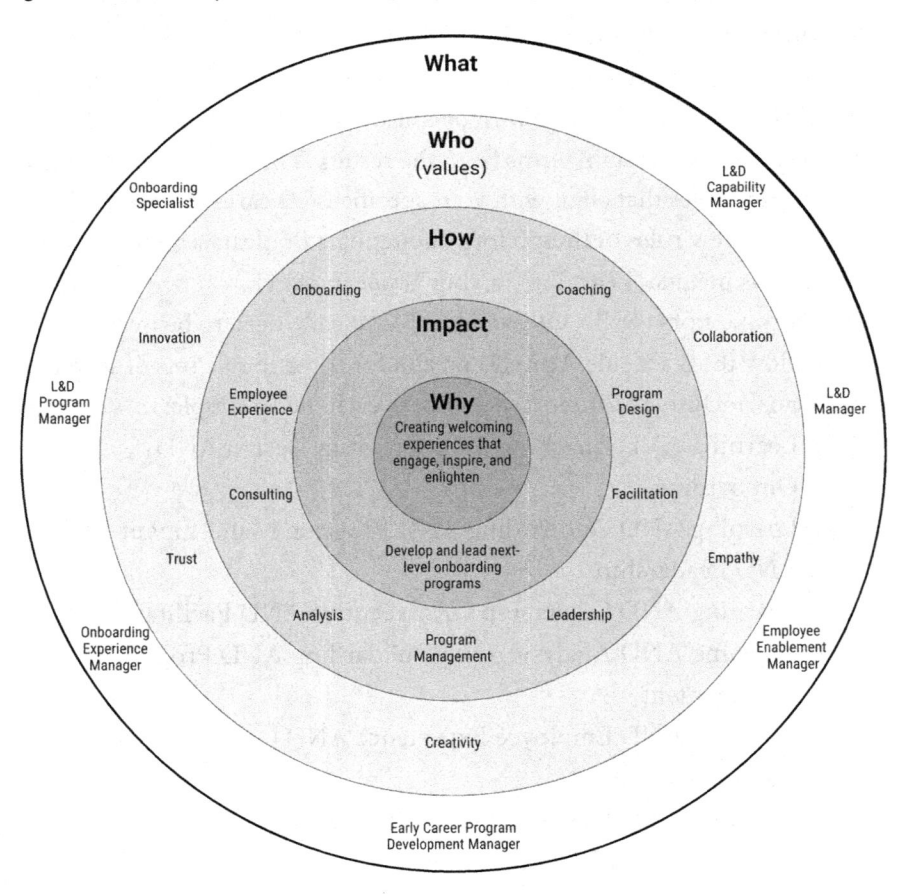

Concentric circle diagram labeled from outside in: What, Who (values), How, Impact, Why.

- **What** (outer ring roles): Onboarding Specialist, L&D Capability Manager, L&D Program Manager, L&D Manager, Onboarding Experience Manager, Employee Enablement Manager, Early Career Program Development Manager
- **Who (values)**: Innovation, Collaboration, Trust, Empathy, Creativity
- **How**: Onboarding, Coaching, Employee Experience, Program Design, Consulting, Facilitation, Analysis, Leadership, Program Management
- **Impact**: Develop and lead next-level onboarding programs
- **Why**: Creating welcoming experiences that engage, inspire, and enlighten

56 • Chapter 4

> **Talent Development Career Pathways Tool**
> In addition to job search sites such as LinkedIn and Indeed, you can use ATD's carer pathway tool to search by skills and identify the type of job family (or families) that most closely align with your L&D niche. Learn more at td.org/career-pathways.

Getting "Proof of Concept"

The last component is getting proof of concept that your L&D niche actually represents what you want to focus on. In the L&D field, it is our job to solve challenges across the organization; however, it's up to you to decide what types of challenges you want to help solve within your niche. This is where networking comes in.

In later chapters, we'll take a deep dive into networking and leveling up your personal brand to create community, but for now we're focusing on networking as a means of data analysis. The best way to find out if you've correctly identified your niche is to find other people who are already in it and learn more about their experiences.

Go to LinkedIn and use the search function to look for people who are in the roles you have listed in the outer edge of your L&D Career Golden Circle (it's OK if your profile isn't built out yet—we'll cover that in chapter 8). Review the profiles that come up, and send a connection request to five to 10 people, with a personalized note such as:

- "I really loved your perspective on [*name*]'s post about [*subject*]. Would love to connect with you to learn more!"
- "Your career journey is really inspiring! I'd love to connect and learn more about how you [*something about their journey*]."
- "I was researching L&D roles to transition into and the role of [*role name*] came up. I see you've been in that role for [*amount of time*] and would love to connect with likeminded people in the space!"

Once you're connected, thank them for accepting your request and ask whether they're open to answering a few questions about their work journey. You can offer to chat over the phone, virtually through Zoom, or even through direct messages on LinkedIn.

Whatever the modality of your conversation, it's important to remember the purpose of this exchange—*for them to share their story so you can determine if you're on the right track with your L&D niche.* It is not for them to give you a job referral or look at your resume or even offer specific advice (unless they willingly offer). Questions you want to ask during these informational interviews include:

- What was your path to get to the role you are in now?
- What does a day-in-the-life look like for you?
- What are the biggest problems and challenges you face in your role?
- What skills are most essential for facing those challenges?

Take note of their answers and start to look for themes and parallels—no two jobs or journeys are exactly the same, but eventually these informational interviews will reveal a pattern in the challenges, skills, and day-to-day activities. Once you do, you can determine whether those challenges, skills, and day-to-day activities excite you. If they do, you've found your niche! If not, that's OK—it just means you'll want to revisit steps three to five and play around with your skills and interests until you find alignment.

> **Let's revisit Debbie:** By doing these exercises, Debbie discovered a burning passion for developing social learning programs and fostering growth and leadership through internal community-building for organizations that valued equity. She took her niche statement, added it to her LinkedIn profile, and developed a resume and personal brand around her L&D niche.
>
> Not long after, Debbie was approached on LinkedIn by a hiring manager from a large, global financial institution committed to equity. They were looking to bring on someone to create social learning programs and build community internally—it couldn't have been more perfect. A few short weeks later, Debbie signed an offer letter as the vice president of digital project management overseeing the strategy and execution of virtual social learning projects and programs, a role she never would have found if she'd kept her focus solely on instructional designer roles.

What's Next? What to Do With an L&D Niche Statement

Now that you have compiled your L&D niche, you'll want to use it as the basis for the next steps of your L&D career transition. Your L&D niche can help you:

- Craft a skills-based, niche-aligned resume and cover letter that doesn't need to be updated for every role (chapter 7).
- Apply to roles that fit within your L&D niche (chapter 4).
- Find other L&D folks within your niche to network with, leverage, learn from, and lean on (chapter 10).
- Create a personal brand and LinkedIn profile that speaks to what you do, how you do it, and who you do it for (chapter 8).
- Prepare for interviews with confidence based on the accomplishments you've gained in previous experiences (chapter 13).

Rather than throwing spaghetti at the wall and hoping something sticks, finding your L&D niche will allow you to expand your career horizons, while providing a framework and path to land the L&D role of your dreams.

Stepping back, when approaching the L&D niche exercise, you can:

- Reflect on your career goals, envision the legacy you want to leave, and identify the specific impact you want to have in your next role.
- Review your career history and identify the skills and interests you want to use in your next role. Be selective and focus on those that energize you and align with your desired impact.
- Combine your legacy, impact, skills, and interests into a cohesive L&D niche statement. This statement will be your North Star that guides your L&D career journey.

SUCCESS CODES A&D

Chapter 5
Motivation, Mindsets, and Habits

"With the right mindset, we can't lose—we either practice what we've learned or we learn what we need to practice." —Noura

When I look back at the more than 1,000 people I've coached over the years, one thing remains constant—*finding a new L&D role is 80 percent mindset and 20 percent strategy*. If you've read the last four chapters, you've probably noticed how, in addition to providing strategic, step-by-step advice to help you find, land, and love your next L&D role, I've woven in techniques to shift your mindset, including intention setting, visualization exercises, and reflection questions.

In her research, Stanford professor and originator of the term *growth mindset*, Carol Dweck (2006) found that when given a difficult task, people with a growth mindset—a belief that abilities and intelligence can be developed through effort, good strategies, and input from others—are far more likely to have success than people with a *fixed mindset*, who are quick to give up. The reality is this: Searching for a new L&D role will always be, in one way or another, a challenging task because it forces you out of your comfort zone. The more you focus on your mindset, motivations, and habits, the more successful you'll find yourself in this process.

The 4 Rs to Reprogram Your Mindset

Whether or not you think you have a growth mindset, the good news is that "a growth mindset is not an innate characteristic, but rather a perspective that can be created and nurtured over time" (Hreha 2023) This means that as long as you are open to consciously shifting your perception, you can develop and nurture a growth mindset. To do so, we'll focus on your career mindset pillars, or the 4 Rs: recommit, reprioritize, rewire, and reconnect (Figure 5-1).

Figure 5-1. The 4Rs

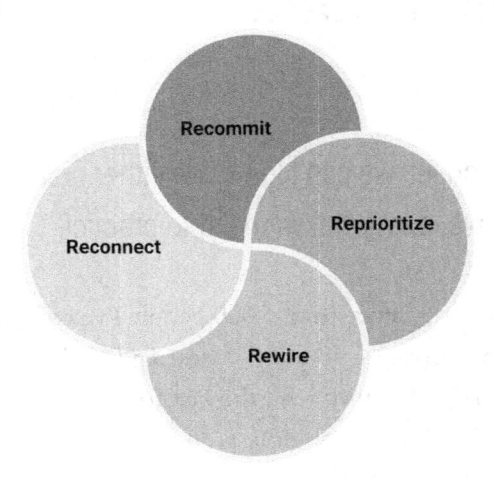

Before we dive into each one, here are a few things to keep in mind:
- While each pillar builds off the next, they are also designed to be focused on individually. Feel free to start with the one that is most relevant to you.
- This is not a one-and-done chapter. While you'll be prompted to complete activities and reflections, creating, growing, and sustaining a growth mindset requires constant attention. I recommend returning to this chapter and its activities regularly.

Pillar 1: Recommit

Recommitting to your goals involves setting clear objectives and regularly checking in on your progress to stay motivated and on track. By creating safe spaces and embracing routine check-ins, you can reinforce your commitment and drive personal growth.

Goal Setting or Audits

In chapter 2, you set intentions and goals aligned with your future career needs and vision. (If you haven't had a chance to read that chapter yet, do that now to ensure you get the most out of this pillar.) Now it's time to recommit to these intentions and goals by reviewing them to ensure they are still in alignment with your career needs and visions.

As you've explored deeper into what types of roles align with you, your intentions or goals may have shifted. To complete your intention or goal audit, ask yourself these questions:

- Are these intentions or goals based on someone else's opinion of how you should spend your time or view your career?
- Did you set these intentions or goals from a place of obligation instead of alignment?
- Are you overwhelmed with how many intentions or goals you've set for yourself?
- Are you confused or unclear as to what your overarching career goal is?
- Have your needs changed?

If you answered yes to any of these questions, it's important to pause. Take some time to rewrite and recommit to this new or shifted set of intentions or goals.

> **Activity**
>
> Reflect on these questions and make any necessary changes and shifts to your intentions or goals:
> - Are these intentions or goals based on someone else's opinion of how I should spend my time or view my career?
> - Did I set these intentions or goals from a place of obligation instead of alignment?
> - Am I overwhelmed with how many intentions or goals I've set for myself?
> - Am I confused or unclear as to what my overarching career goal is?
> - Have my needs changed?

Once you've reviewed and reflected on your current intentions and goals, recommit to them by taking these steps:
1. **Revisit your why.** In several previous chapters, you identified your motivation for finding a new L&D role. Take a few moments to recommit to this motivation.
2. **Assess what you've already accomplished.** Review the parts of your goals you've already started working on. Celebrate any progress you've made toward living these intentions or goals.
3. **Identify what is getting in your way.** If your intentions and goals are aligned, but you're still struggling with them, look at what may be getting in your way. The rest of this chapter will also help you take inventory of any roadblocks stopping you from achieving your goals.

Creating Safe Spaces

Have you ever wanted to get started on a new project or felt super energized to check something off your list, only to become overwhelmed by the space you're in? You may notice how easy it is for that overwhelm to creep into your project and consume any energy you had to check off that task. This is a cycle that many people fall into, because "our outerworlds invariably affect our inner worlds, and vice versa" (Silva 2023).

Your Physical Space

According to a study conducted by the Princeton Neuroscience Institute, "having multiple visual stimuli present within range of one's view will result in those stimuli competing for neural representation." In other words, the more clutter you can see, the more easily you'll get distracted. That's not to say your space needs to be pristine before you can be productive; in fact, some people work best with a little organized chaos (myself included). You simply need to create a physical space that sets you up for success.

To do this, you'll first need to take inventory of your spaces. When you look at your intentions and goals, in what environment are you making them come to life? If you're in the midst of a career transition, where are you doing most of that work? If your intention for work-life balance is to make sure you can continue to work out, where are you keeping your workout clothes and equipment? Before you audit the physical spaces, you need to identify them.

Once you've done that, you can reflect on how to improve these physical spaces by asking yourself a few questions about each space:
- What are you physically holding on to in this space that is no longer serving your intentions?
- How do you want to feel when you walk into this space? What is one thing you can do today to make this space feel that way?
- What do you need to change about this space to inspire you to achieve your goals?
- How can you commit to keeping this space in alignment with your intentions and goals?

Meet Rebecca: As a remote vice president of L&D, Rebecca spent hundreds upon hundreds of hours in her home office working for an organization that didn't align with her values. Tired of being overworked, overlooked, and not supported, Rebecca made the decision to leave her role in pursuit of a new opportunity. However, every time Rebecca sat down to work on her job search, she immediately got a pit in her stomach and couldn't 100 percent focus on the task at hand. Something needed to change.

So, after asking herself some questions to reflect on her physical space, she realized that nothing about her desk setup had changed since she'd left that toxic work environment. As a result, her body's muscle memory immediately went into fight or flight mode as soon as she sat down.

Rebecca needed to cleanse her space! She removed old papers she didn't need and rearranged the room. She put her desk under two big windows, added a chair from a different room, removed a big piece of furniture, and created an at home library using bookshelves she already had. This new space no longer reminded her of her previous toxic work environment—now it inspired her to achieve her goals.

Activity
It's your turn to take inspired action and cleanse your physical spaces. Review these reflection questions, and pick a physical space to begin auditing:
- What am I physically holding on to in this space that is no longer serving my intentions?

- How do I want to feel when I walk into this space? What is one thing I can do today to make this space feel that way?
- What do I need to change about this space to inspire me to achieve my goals?
- How can I commit to keeping this space in alignment with my intentions and goals?

If a space is already serving you as-is, feel free to move on to the next section.

Your Digital Space

If you're anything like me, you have a lot of digital real estate. Documents, files, music, emails, apps, social media—the list goes on. As with your physical spaces, your digital spaces can often, and very quickly, become cluttered. According to Cal Newport (2019), author of *Digital Minimalism*, "this is why [digital] clutter is dangerous. It's easy to be seduced by the small amounts of profit offered by the latest app or service, but then forget its cost in terms of the most important resource we possess: the minutes of our life." While the world we live in creates limitless opportunities to access digital information, the flip side of this digital abundance is that it becomes incredibly easy to feel overwhelmed and burned out from it all.

Your digital spaces can be broken down into six distinct categories: documents, emails and inbox, social media, news, apps and programs, and passwords. Similar to your physical spaces, you'll need to conduct a digital space inventory by identifying any areas of digital clutter causing you stress or preventing you from embodying your intentions. For example, you might have dozens of documents saved on your desktop, an overflowing email inbox, or a social media account that's causing a lot of distraction.

After you've identified your digital spaces, reflect on how to improve them by asking yourself these questions for each space:
- How do you want to feel when you use this digital space? What is one thing you can do today to make this space feel that way?
- What do you need to change about this digital space to inspire you to achieve your goals?
- How can you commit to keeping this space in alignment with your intentions and goals?

Activity

It's your turn to take inspired action and cleanse your digital spaces. Review these reflection questions, and pick one digital space at a time to begin auditing:
- How do I want to feel when I use this digital space? What is one thing I can do today to make this space feel that way?
- What do I need to change about this digital space to inspire me to achieve my goals?
- How can I commit to keeping this space in alignment with my intentions and goals?

If a space is already serving you as-is, feel free to move on to the next section.

Tips and Best Practices for Recommitting

- **Remember, it's OK for your goals and intentions to shift.** As you start to grow, evolve, and learn more about your career needs and desires, it's perfectly normal for your goals to evolve as well.
- **Have fun with your physical and digital space cleanse!** Get creative with how you organize (for example, the folder on my desktop for all my book writing is titled "Woohoo You're Writing a Book!" which is much more fun than just labeling it "Book Stuff"). Put on your favorite podcast, playlist, or audiobook to keep you entertained while you work.
- **Make sure you celebrate.** After cleansing each space, give yourself a little celebration or reward. Perhaps you take a night off to watch TV or buy a little something to add to your cleansed space—it's up to you!

Pillar 2: Reprioritize

Recommitting to our intentions and goals is a great first step to boosting our mindset and motivation, but if we don't prioritize those intentions and goals, they may get lost or forgotten. So, we need to build sustainable systems and structures through our habits and hobbies to reprioritize our goals and intentions.

Habits provide structure and routine in your daily life, helping to bring your intentions to life, whereas *hobbies* offer creative outlets, reduce stress, and enhance overall well-being. Prioritizing both habits and hobbies is the key to sustained success.

Habitual Systems and Structures

Your intention-led goals only get you so far without the right structures to support them. In chapter 2, we introduced this intention and corresponding goal:
- Intention: I maintain a work-life balance.
- Goal: Schedule one to two "me-time" activities each week.

You may have every intention of achieving that goal, but if you don't have a habitual system or structure in place, it's easy to forget those me-time activities or push them to the side. While you may think (and hope) you'll get to it later, the more you deviate from your real priorities, the harder it is to remember they exist. In fact, later may never come, and you'll be left wondering why you're not any closer to achieving your goals or living out your intentions.

The way to break this cycle is to create a system and structure to support your intentions and goals. Take a look at each of your intentions, and ask yourself this question: *The "me" who embodies my intentions has what habits to support them?*

For example, someone who embodies the intention of "I maintain a work-life balance," with the goal of "scheduling one to two me-time activities each week," may create a habitual system or structure to review their calendar weekly and block off and plan for their me-time.

> **Activity**
> Review your intentions and goals. What habitual structures and systems do you need to put in place to support them?

Conscious Commitment

While there is a lot of conflicting research on how long it takes to actually develop a habit or form a new system or structure, we can all agree that it doesn't happen overnight. In fact, it starts with a conscious commitment that eventually has the potential to become second nature. Creating the structure isn't enough—you must commit to it.

Conscious commitment is all about setting your structure up for success. For example, if someone's habitual system or structure is to review their calendar weekly and block off and plan for me-time a week in advance, they may need to make the conscious commitment to set an alarm reminding them to do that activity every Sunday evening.

> **Activity**
> Now that you've identified your habitual structures and systems, what commitments will you make to set them up for success?

Hobbies

Think back to the times in your career when you were faced with an overwhelming challenge? What was the first thing you put aside to focus on that? Most likely, it was a hobby.

My hobby is reading, and I read voraciously (usually at least one book a week). For a few weeks, as I was writing *this* book, I didn't read a single page. One day, as I sat at my desk typing, I wondered why I was feeling a bit uninspired—and then it hit me that I wasn't prioritizing my source of stress relief: reading. In fact, I actually felt guilty about reading if I had a deadline coming up, so told myself I'd read again as a reward for finishing this book. I immediately shut down my computer, grabbed a book I had been dying to read, and read the entire thing in two days. Then, I went back to my computer with a renewed sense of energy and excitement—all because I reprioritized a hobby that enhanced my well-being.

> **Activity**
> Reflect on what brings you energy, relieves stress, and enhances your overall well-being. Have you been actively prioritizing these things? If not, what hobby can you commit to reprioritizing this week?

Tips and Best Practices for Reprioritizing

- **Try to habit stack.** Developed by BJ Fogg and popularized by James Clear, the idea of habit stacking is simple: Rather than pairing your new habit with a particular time and location, you pair it with a current habit.
- **Do things one at a time.** Whenever you're introducing new habits, structures, systems, and even hobbies, it's easy to burn yourself out if you try to change everything at once. Instead, start with one new habit, and incrementally add on from there.
- **Practice, not perfection, is the goal.** Forget your habit one day? It's OK! You won't stop brushing your teeth for the rest of your life because you fell asleep one night without doing it—same goes for your goals. Show yourself grace and pick up where you left off.

Pillar 3: Rewire

Your thoughts can create your reality. According to *Psychology Today*: "Your thoughts, if you think them over and over, and assign truth to them, become beliefs. Beliefs create a cognitive lens through which you interpret the events of your world and this lens serves as a selective filter through which you sift the environment for evidence that matches up with what you believe to be true."

In chapter 3, we looked at how your root source thoughts could help you gain clarity and confidence in your new L&D career journey, no matter what prompted it. Now, we'll build on the concepts in that chapter and explore a self-coaching model to apply if you notice those thoughts creeping up to the surface and influencing your ability to embody your intentions.

Our thoughts are wired to protect us. While understanding the root source of our thoughts requires a conscious and constant effort, the more we're able to notice those thoughts rise and acknowledge them as protection, the easier it becomes to flip the script on them. This is particularly important because no two days will feel the same, regardless of where you are in navigating your L&D career. How you learn to manage your thoughts will ultimately determine your success.

Our thoughts are triggered by emotions. Throughout each day, we experience conscious emotions we can observe, as well as micro-emotions that may pass us by without us even noticing. While you may not recognize these micro-emotions, your brain catches on to them and uses them to trigger thoughts. Have you ever had a random thought pop in your head but you didn't know why? Most likely, it was triggered by a micro-emotion.

Throughout your L&D career journey, you are bound to experience a rollercoaster of emotions and micro-emotions that bring potentially intrusive thoughts to the forefront of your mind. When those intrusive thoughts take hold, they have an immediate and direct influence on your feelings, which in turn determines the actions you take, which then influences your overall results. Those results typically reinforce your original thoughts, and the cycle continues (Figure 5-2).

Figure 5-2. The Cycle From Thoughts to Results

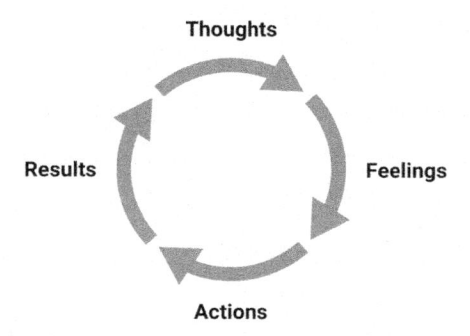

Thoughts → Feelings → Actions → Results → (cycle)

Meet Luke: During our time working together, Luke experienced a lot of ups and downs. The organization they were working at was grossly misaligned with their core values, and every day was another battle through endless emotions and micro-emotions. This bled over in their job search, and after receiving a few back-to-back rejections for L&D roles they really wanted, Luke's thoughts took over.

I remember them saying, "I'm never going to get out of this job." The more Luke let that thought sink in, the more they started to feel hopeless, depressed, and lethargic, which led them to procrastinate, isolate from our coaching group, and mass apply to roles they didn't even want. The results? Even more rejections, perpetuating Luke's thoughts that they would never get out of their job.

So how did Luke break the cycle and land their dream role in the L&D space? By using a flipped model of self-coaching (Figure 5-3). To self-coach out of an intrusive thought, you first have to recognize that the thought is occurring. As soon as it travels across your mind, it's up to you to pause and focus on rewriting that thought narrative and returning to your intentions.

Once you've recognized that intrusive thought, you'll want to choose an intention most closely related to the thought you're experiencing. Remember, your intentions are the results you want to embody, so you need to flip the cycle and start with the results. Once you've selected an intention, you need to identify the actions that someone who embodies that intention takes, and how those actions feel. Finally, you'll reflect on the thoughts someone (you) who embodies those actions has.

Figure 5-3. The Cycle From Results to Thoughts

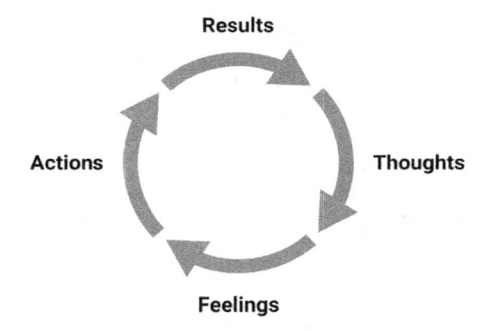

> Luke was ready for a shift in perspective and revisited their intentions—specifically "I'm surrounded by diverse people, thoughts, and perspectives." The actions of someone with that intention reminded Luke of their natural ability to seek out and build a diverse network, leaving them feeling proud and inspired. Luke's feeling of inspiration led them to the thought, "it's possible to find a new work environment that celebrates diversity." By noticing as soon as that intrusive thought crossed their mind, Luke was able to neutralize it.

> **Activity**
> Recall the last intrusive thoughts that led you away from your intentions. How did they influence your feelings, actions, and results? How would you self-coach through those thoughts and flip the model?

Keep this in mind as you practice self-coaching—the idea is not to immediately shift from a negative to a positive thought (in doing so too quickly, you may be gaslighting yourself). Instead, the concept of self-coaching allows you to neutralize the thought. In Luke's case, the intrusive thought of "I'm never going to get out of this job" was not replaced with a more positive thought of "I'll be out of here soon." Instead, it was neutralized by the new thought of "it's possible to find a new work environment that celebrates diversity."

Tips and Best Practices for Rewiring

- **Practice mindfulness.** How many thoughts race through your head in a day without you pausing to assess if they are helping or harming your mindset? Make sure to take some daily mindful moments to check in with your emotions, micro-emotions, and thoughts.
- **Keep track of your thoughts.** Keep a small notebook nearby and practice cataloging your thoughts throughout the day. Then, choose one to focus on rewiring.
- **Focus on embodying feelings and actions.** Consider the actions and feelings that are aligned with your intentions. How can you embody them today, even if you don't completely have your desired result yet?

Pillar 4: Reconnect

The most important person in your career journey is you. If you have lost connection with yourself, it will be almost impossible to find fulfillment in your career because you'll always be focused on what others expect of you rather than what you expect of yourself.

Antoinette Njombua-Fombad (2021), connection and awareness coach and founder of WITHIN, describes self-connection as when "we start to contribute as who we are rather than who we should be, and the world starts to receive us as such rather than what it expects of us."

If you've gone through the previous three pillars (thoroughly) you should be starting to feel a sense of self-connectedness. That's because each time we reconnect with our intentions, goals, habits, hobbies, and thought processes, we become more connected to our sense of self.

Reconnecting and staying connected to yourself requires the same conscious commitment we discussed in pillar 2. The self-love wheel depicts seven areas we should assess and focus on when assessing our own self-love:

- **Mindfulness.** Live in the present moment and stay fully engaged; accept what's happening in your surroundings.
- **Self-care.** Take as best care as possible of your basic needs and make sure you're nurtured, including but not limited to proper nutrition, exercise, sleep, and so on.
- **Boundaries.** Set limits or say no to things that deplete or harm you physically, emotionally, or mentally.
- **Self-forgiveness.** Accept your humanity by practicing being less hard on yourself when you make a mistake so you can focus on lessons learned instead.
- **Gratitude.** The self-love hack is practicing gratitude. Research has shown repeatedly that practicing gratitude reduces stress, anxiety, depression, and pain, and builds an overall sense of satisfaction and esteem.
- **People.** Surround yourself with people who cheer you on, pick you up when you fall, and see and respect you for who you are. (More on this in chapter 10.)
- **Self-awareness.** Have an in-depth understanding of your thoughts, feelings, and behaviors, and how they are connected; recognize your strengths, weaknesses, and emotional triggers.

Figure 5-4 provides an example of how someone might fill in their self-love wheel.

Figure 5-4. The Self-Love Wheel

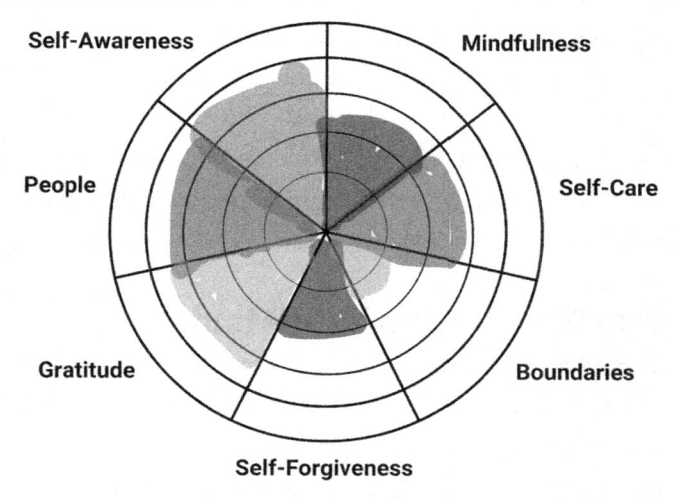

Self-Awareness, Mindfulness, Self-Care, Boundaries, Self-Forgiveness, Gratitude, People

Activity
Reflect on how the version of you who fully embodies your intentions shows self-love. Once you've defined each area for yourself, use the self-love wheel to shade in your current level for your self-love journey.

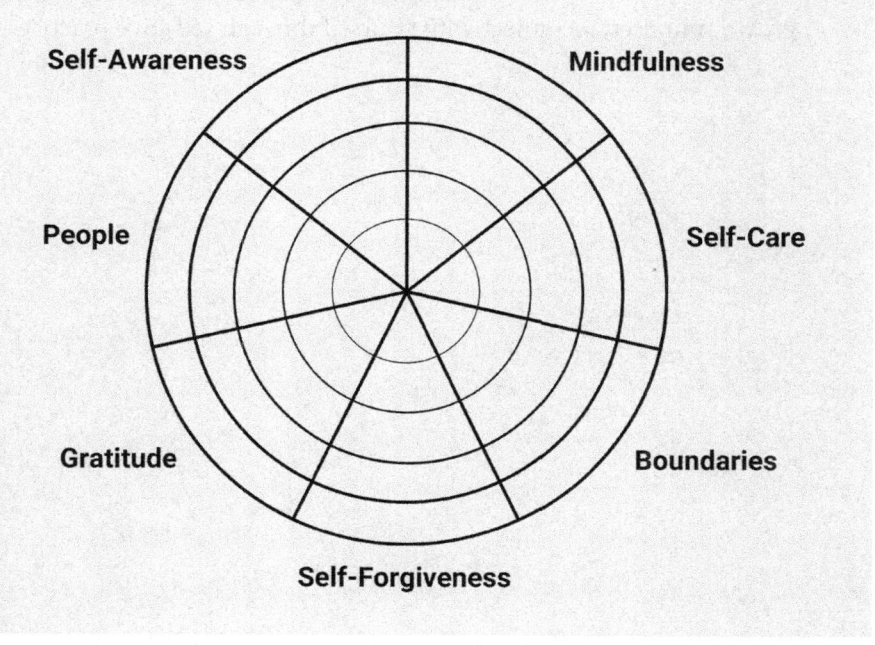

Motivation, Mindsets, and Habits 75

Tips and Best Practices for Reconnecting
- **It's a journey, not a destination.** As with many concepts in this book, this is not a one-and-done practice. To really cultivate self-love, you'll need to come back to these exercises often.
- **Daily commitment is key.** Make a habit of intentionally showing yourself self-love every day. Choose from one of the seven self-love areas and practice as often as you can.

What's Next? Resetting Your Mindset

Your mindset determines the success and direction of your career. Before moving on with any more tactical job search actions, consider pausing and focusing on the following:
- Review and adjust your career intentions and goals to make sure they align with your current vision and career needs. Create physical and digital spaces that help you meet those needs.
- Identify and implement habits in support of your intentions, focusing on reintroducing and prioritizing hobbies that bring you joy.
- Practice self-coaching to manage intrusive thoughts and cultivate a growth mindset; reconnect with yourself through self-love practices.

PART 2
Positioning Yourself in the L&D Market

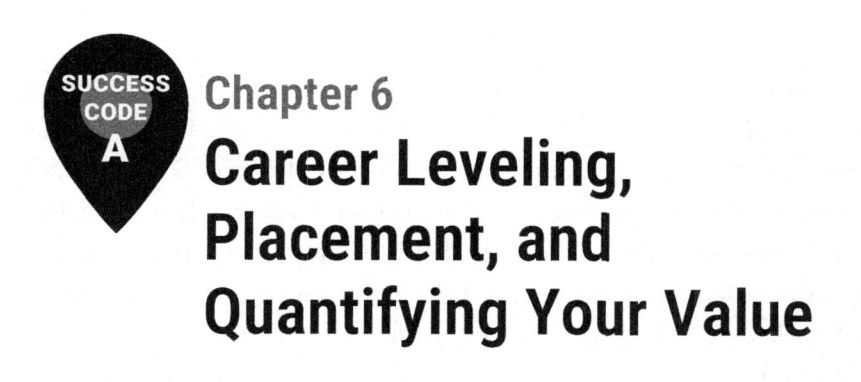

Chapter 6
Career Leveling, Placement, and Quantifying Your Value

"If you don't value yourself, then you will always be attracted to people who don't value you either." —Sabrina Alexis

So, you've figured out what the right role looks like for you at the right company, but how do you know if it's the right level for you? One of the most common internal challenges I've observed in L&D job hunts is the struggle to determine the right level and salary.

The Qualification Goldilocks Effect
If all L&D job titles were created equal, it would be much easier to identify which roles job seekers are qualified for. Given that they're not (yet), it's easy to get caught up in the L&D job Goldilocks effect of navigating what you are overqualified for, underqualified for, and where your qualifications are just right.

While there is no exact science for determining the appropriate job level to seek next, it's important to understand the implications of falling into overqualified or underqualified territory. According to a 2008 study by *The International Journal of Human Resource Management*, there is a direct correlation between those who are cognitively aware they are overqualified for their role and overall job dissatisfaction. In addition, while the exact likelihood is not quantified, hiring managers perceive a risk of higher, faster turnover among overqualified hires compared with candidates they believe are appropriately qualified.

There are many reasons people apply for and seek out roles for which they are overqualified, but the number 1 reason has less to do with circumstances and more to do with confidence. In fact, a recent study of 2,000 US job seekers by the Adecco Group found that 39 percent fear potential employers would deem them underqualified for the roles they are applying for, even though they meet the qualifications (SWNS 2023). This creates a unique paradox—when job seekers fear they are underqualified, they apply for roles they are actually overqualified for and are then perceived as a hiring risk by the hiring manager who is looking for someone more appropriately qualified. It can, unfortunately, turn into a never-ending cycle of rejection, further demoralizing you as a job seeker.

If we know that being overqualified for a role will likely turn off a hiring manager and increase the likelihood of job dissatisfaction, why would anyone apply for a role if they are overqualified for it (aside from the fear we've already discussed)?

- **Work-life harmony.** In many roles, the higher you rise, the more pressures you face, which may in-turn disrupt your work-life harmony. Some people make a conscious decision to apply to roles they are overqualified for in hopes of reducing workload and pressure. If you are in this boat, keep in mind that this may be a reflection of organizational culture rather than appropriate leveling. Before you decide to seek a role you are overqualified for, do some preliminary research to identify if the pressure you are experiencing is typical for your level, or if it is caused your organization's culture. If it's cultural, you may find that you simply need to shift your focus to finding an organization that aligns with how you value work-life harmony.
- **Lifestyle preferences and changes.** The work we do should positively influence our lifestyle preferences and changes; in some cases, it benefits job seekers to apply for roles that best accommodate their lifestyle, even if they're overqualified. For example, you may need a more fluid schedule, or have to work part-time while caretaking for family, or decide to try your hand in something completely new through a temporary assignment or contract.

- **Underemployed or unemployed.** During economic downturns or periods of high unemployment, overqualified job seekers may find themselves applying for lower-level roles out of necessity until better prospects arise. However, employment expert and author of *Agile Unemployment*, Sabina Sulat (2021), warns that one of the main downsides of accepting a role you're overqualified for "is the risk of becoming stuck in a position that does not fully utilize your skills and experiences. This can lead to feelings of frustration, and boredom that can hinder professional development and job performance."

While we will discuss interviews in later chapters, it's important to prepare yourself now to answer questions regarding your level of experience and what prompted you to apply for this level role. Some questions overqualified job seekers may get asked include:

1. What motivates you to take a step back in terms of responsibilities or seniority?
2. How will you remain engaged in this role given your experience level?
3. Are you willing to work within the set pay range for this position despite your experience level?
4. How will you adapt to a role with potentially less autonomy or authority than you're accustomed to?

While there are challenges when it comes to being overqualified, the same can be said for applying to roles you are underqualified for. While you don't need to meet 100 percent of the qualifications to apply for a role (we'll get into that a little later in this chapter), there is a fine line between a role being a stretch and one you are not qualified to be doing. According to Robert Half (2019), on average, 42 percent of all submitted applications are from candidates who don't meet the job requirements, which means if you are underqualified for a role, you're likely competing against a majority of candidates who are appropriately qualified.

Finding the Alignment Sweet Spot

Here are some ways to ensure you're applying for roles that are most aligned with your skills, interests, experience, and expertise:

1. **Go beyond job titles.** As we discussed in chapter 4, L&D job titles are open to interpretation—meaning that you can't judge a job by its title. So, when you're doing your job search, make sure to spend time reviewing each job description carefully. While it takes some extra time upfront, it will ensure that you are clear on the job expectations before applying and hoping for the best.
2. **Match your experience to the job responsibilities.** Each job description outlines the expectations you will be responsible for. As you review each responsibility, ask, "Where does this align with my education, experience, skills, or other qualifications?" A good rule of thumb is that your experience should align with at least 70 percent of the listed responsibilities.
3. **Distinguish between required and preferred qualifications.** It's important to pay attention to the language that's used in job descriptions. Many will use specific terms to indicate to potential candidates the qualifications they would like to see in the person they choose to hire, such as required or preferred qualifications:
    - *Required qualifications.* If a job description uses the terms *required, minimum,* or *basic* to describe a corresponding list of qualifications, you want to ensure you meet 90 percent, if not all, of them. While you may still choose to apply for the role, keep in mind that by using these terms, the job poster is intentionally seeking a candidate who meets those qualifications at a minimum.
    - *Preferred qualifications.* If a job description uses the terms *preferred* or *desired* to describe a list of qualifications, it's relatively safe to say that, while valued by the employer, those qualifications are not mandatory. Because preferred qualifications demonstrate experience, education, or skills beyond the minimum requirements, you ideally want to possess a combination of both. I like to think of preferred qualifications as a holiday wish list—we know we are not going to get everything we ask for, but we'll be really happy if we receive a good chunk of that list. For preferred qualifications, you want to aim to meet 70 percent or higher, although this can be a little more fluid.

4. **Consider equivalent and transferable experience.** This is where many job seekers sell themselves short—they don't consider the weight their transferable experience holds. While most job descriptions have required and preferred qualifications, they don't always have to be one-to-one comparisons. For example, prior to my career in talent development, I was a sales manager for a large real estate organization. In my role as a sales manager, I was coaching employees on sales techniques, creating how-to guides, facilitating sales training sessions for my team, and recording short videos on how to use our proprietary software. When it came time to raise my hand for a new L&D role inside the organization, my transferable and equivalent experience made me a prime candidate for the role even though I didn't have years of traditional TD experience.
5. **Pay attention to the order.** While there isn't a universally accepted or research-backed order that job descriptions follow, they tend to list the most important qualifications first, followed by the hiring manager's interpretation of the nice-to-haves. Again, this is not an exact science, but it's something to pay attention to as you weigh qualifications.

Something else I share with my L&D career coaching clients is that your dream job is the job that gives you the runway to live your dream life, not the other way around. With the qualification spectrum in mind, it's important to also consider your life circumstances when career leveling. Examples of this include not wanting a high-pressure role so you can shut off at the end of the day, choosing not to manage a team so you can focus solely on being an individual contributor, or applying for a role that gives you flexibility to manage a health issue. On the flip side, you may pursue a high-pressure role with a high salary (although high pressure and high salary are not mutually exclusive) to put yourself in a prime financial position, or you may decide to pivot to a new industry or type of role that better suits your long-term goals. When it comes to appropriate leveling, make sure to consider both your qualifications and your life circumstances.

Activity
Reflect on a job you recently applied for. Write down how well your skills, experience, and life circumstances aligned with the job description.
- Did you consider all aspects like job responsibilities, required and preferred qualifications, and your personal needs?
- What would you do differently in your next job search to ensure better alignment?

Meet Lisa: When Lisa and I began working together in the fall of 2021, she had been on her L&D job search for a few months without any success. As a former educator turned communications strategist turned employee experience specialist, Lisa had an arsenal of skills and experience but was stuck in a cycle of underselling herself by applying for more entry-level L&D roles. She had a rich background in developing learning content and curriculum (from her K–12 education roles), crafting compelling internal and external messaging and copy (from her communication and copy editing role), and creating DEI-fueled employee experiences and programs. As we began to unpack her true qualifications, Lisa shifted her focus from applying solely to entry-level L&D positions to roles where she could use the high-level experience she'd gained in her more nontraditional TD roles.

Lisa also considered the quality of life she wanted to have, which included being financially able to travel to her favorite destination, Paris, more often. In addition to seeking out a role aligned with her high-level skills, she also factored in the financial position she would need to be in to create the life of her dreams and what that looked like in terms of leveling. After recalibrating and applying to the higher-level L&D roles she was appropriately qualified for, Lisa landed an L&D leadership position at a technology company—and celebrated by taking a trip to Paris before she started.

Talent Development Career Pathways Tool
To get a peek into the different level types and associated skills for specific L&D job facilities, check out the ATD career pathways tool. Learn more at td.org/career-pathways.

Quantifying Your Value

So you've successfully identified the right level for you based on your experience and qualifications, but how do you quantify it? Do you have a number in mind for when you inevitably get asked, "What salary range are you targeting?" (More on how to appropriately answer that question in chapter 13.)

Long gone are the days when talking about salary in the beginning of the interview process was considered taboo; talking about it early on and advocating for what you're worth is now the norm. But how can you advocate for yourself if you're not clear on the number? How do you make sure you don't sell yourself short? How do you ensure the number you're targeting is realistic? Take a three-pronged approach by looking at what you need to make, your market value, and your experience value (Figure 6-1).

Figure 6-1. The Three-Pronged Approach to Finding Your Salary Range

What You Need to Make

Remember, your mindset in finding and landing your next L&D role is that this is the job that gives you the runway to live your dream life, not the other way around. So as you begin to think about quantifying your value, you need to start by identifying the salary that will support your current lifestyle and that you hope your next job will allow you to afford. This includes calculating your basic necessities, including rent or mortgage, additional living expenses, pet care, car and transportation costs, student loan payments, childcare, groceries, taxes, and personal and healthcare expenses.

In addition, you'll want to calculate your desired needs, such as entertainment, travel, discretionary spending, subscriptions, memberships, a monthly savings goal, and nonessential personal care (including gym memberships, massages, haircuts, manicures, and so on). The goal is to account for anything that aligns with the life you desire to live (within reason because your next job likely won't afford you the ability to buy a private jet). Create a full picture of what your life looks like when you have the means to afford it, and remember this is a deeply personal number that no algorithm can decide for you.

> **Activity**
>
> Take a few moments to reflect on your current lifestyle, and the one you hope your next job will allow you to afford. Calculate the costs of your basic necessities, alongside your desired needs, and annualize that number.

Your Market Value

In chapter 4, you adapted Simon Sinek's Golden Circle to create your own L&D career golden circle. You started outlining the types of job titles that align with your skills, interests, and values in your circle's outer rim. Now, it's time to revisit those job titles in combination with the knowledge you've gained about leveling to begin identifying the market value of the roles aligned with your niche. Using a tool like Salary.com, begin to research different job titles. Take note of the different filters you can use including location, years of experience, and direct reports.

Note: You may need to shift some titles around when searching for salary info in online databases. As an example, "director of learning and development" wasn't listed on Salary.com, but the next closest role, "training director," was. I recommend doing this exercise for at least four of the job titles in your L&D niche.

Once you've gathered a handful of salaries for roles that align with your L&D niche, calculate the average salary across all of them. This number is the market value of your L&D niche. Then, compare your market value number with your what-you-need-to-make number. If it's the same or higher, you've leveled appropriately and are aligned. If, however, if your market value is lower than what you need to make, you will have to reassess your niche or your level, or both.

> **Activity**
> Revisit the job titles you identified in your L&D career golden circle and select at least four to search for on Salary.com or another tool. Use your findings to calculate your L&D niche's market value.

Your Experience Value

While calculating the market value and what you need to make are typically more objective, coming up with a salary number to represent your experience is harder. Here are a few things to think about when determining the value of your experience:

- **Related education and certifications.** What do you consider the value-add that your relevant education and certifications bring to the table? For example, if you have a master's degree in a relevant or related field, consider the cost of that education and how that factors into the return on your investment.
- **Previous expertise.** What do you consider to be the value of your previous expertise and experience? If you've been able to increase productivity or save a previous organization a significant amount of money by activating your skill set, calculate what that may be worth to your future employer.
- **Value of your time.** Imagine yourself a year from now. What salary made this type of work worth your time? While it may be appealing to settle for any reasonable salary, it's important to factor in the value of your time and consider what will feel aligned after the initial allure and onboarding of a new job wears off.

> **Activity**
> Calculate your experience value by determining what salary range aligns with your education, certifications, previous expertise, and time value.

Now that you have all three numbers, you can start putting together your ideal salary range. To calculate the bottom of your range, take the average of

all three numbers. To calculate the top end of your range, take your highest number and add about 5 percent to it. Here's an example:
- What you need to make: $106,000
- Market value: $140,000
- Experience value: $130,000
- Range bottom: $125,000
- Range top: $147,000

Now that you have your salary range, you may also want to consider how much of that you need or want in cash compensation versus what you are willing to accept in additional forms of compensation. Some additional forms of compensation include:

- **Bonuses.** Additional cash payments can reward performance, goal achievement, or company profits. These may be paid out annually, quarterly, or monthly depending on the organization.
- **Profit sharing.** In some cases, employees of certain companies may receive a portion of the company's profits.
- **Equity compensation.** At many publicly traded organizations employees are allowed to purchase company shares at a set price or are given stock grants.
- **Cash allowances.** These are nontaxable cash amounts for specific expenses like relocation, a home office, and gym membership reimbursement.

Activity
Using the three values you just determined—what you need to make, your market value, and your experience value—calculate the top and bottom of your salary range. Consider how much of that amount you want to receive through cash compensation, or what, if any, you are willing to accept in additional forms of compensation. Remember, this is not an exact science, but it will help provide a window into your ideal compensation band.

What's Next? Determining Your Career Level

Having a range in mind will be incredibly helpful when reviewing job descriptions (as many display their budgeted salary in the job description, with some states requiring it). It also allows you to go into interviews feeling confident about your worth and market value. Taking the time to get clarity on the most appropriate level and market value will set you up for success in being able to identify the right roles to start pursuing. Remember these tips:

- Reflect on your current qualifications and determine if you're aiming for roles that you are appropriately qualified for, avoiding the pitfalls of being overqualified or underqualified. Remember, you should aim to meet around 70 percent of preferred qualifications and 90 to 100 percent of required qualifications.
- Calculate your ideal salary range by considering your current and desired lifestyle, the market value of roles in your L&D niche, and the value of your experience, education, and certifications.
- Ensure your career decisions align with your broader life goals and circumstances, such as work-life harmony, financial stability, and personal growth.

SUCCESS CODES A & B

Chapter 7
Creating Your Niche-Aligned Resume and Cover Letter

"The challenge of life, I have found, is to build a resume that doesn't simply tell a story about what you want to be, but it's a story about who you want to be." —Oprah Winfrey

I imagine there are three types of people reading this chapter right now—those of you who rushed here before reading the rest of the book because you're eager to get your resume out in the world, those of you who arrived here because you're reading the book from cover to cover, and those of you who put this chapter off as long as possible because of the mountain of anxiety that comes along with creating yet another resume.

No matter which camp you are in, I'm here to tell you that we're about to change everything you've ever known about writing a resume.

The Marketing Mindset Shift

Before we dive into creating a resume that will land you interview after interview, you need to shift your perspective. Most people approach resume writing by trying to create a digital collection of everything they've ever done in their careers. However, your resume is actually a marketing document that highlights what you want to do next through the lens of what you've done in the past. It serves as a promotional tool to showcase your capabilities to a future employer.

Think of it as any advertisement. If you see a Nike ad on a billboard, in a magazine, or on social media, what you won't find is a laundry list of all the materials used to make its shoes, or details about where each component came from. You won't see any mention of who designed the shoe, or information about the factory where it was produced—because none of that is relevant to the end consumer. What you will see is what Nike wants you, the consumer, to do with its shoe—run faster, jump higher, climb farther. The same goes for your resume—what do you want the end consumer, the hiring manager or recruiter, to be able to do with you on their team?

This requires shifting your mindset. You will have to be particular about what you want to showcase on your resume and the story you want to tell.

The One-and-Done Resume Methodology

How many times have you been told to "tailor your resume to each job you are applying for"? I'll bet it's more than a few. Unfortunately, it's one of the most harmful pieces of resume advice you can follow.

Gasp. I know—but hear me out.

In chapter 4, we explored the importance of finding your L&D niche—the intersection of your skills, interests, and values that describe what you want to do next (impact), how you want to do it (skills and interests), and for what type of company (values). If every role you apply to requires a drastic update to your resume, that indicates one of two things:

- **You're not clear on your niche.** If every role is so different, it's time to pause and ask yourself if you're shooting at a moving target in the dark. The less clear you are on what the right role at the right company looks like for you, the more likely you'll be to update your resume for each job, because they all seem doable.
- **You're casting too wide a net.** You may have clearly defined your niche, but you're operating outside it using a spray and pray mentality. One thing to keep in mind is that the rule of averages does not apply to job applications. The number of jobs you apply to does not correlate with the number of interviews you go on.

You may be asking yourself, "Don't employers want to see a tailored resume?" The answer isn't black and white. Employers want to see that you can do the job they are hiring for, and that you have the experience to back it up. What they don't want to see is their job description regurgitated back to them in the form of a resume. Hyper-fixating on tailoring your resume is the quickest way to remove its authenticity.

The other issue with tailoring your resume is that everyone else is doing it (it is the number 1 piece of resume advice, after all). So, rather than standing out, you end up blending in with the sea of applicants all using the same exact keywords, phrases, and skill sets. In addition, you may unknowingly remove a skill the hiring manager didn't even know they were looking for.

In one of my previous roles as a training director, I opened a requisition for an instructional designer to join my team. More than 300 candidates applied within a week. The company had a small HR team, so I was responsible for going through each and every resume. They all started to blend together—until one stood out in particular. While that resume aligned with the experience I was looking for, it also showcased specific skills outside traditional instructional design, with the most eye-catching skill being "creative writing." That wasn't a skill I was initially seeking out in this next hire, but I couldn't stop thinking about how helpful creative writing ability would be on the team, and suddenly, no other resume really compared. By staying true to her unique skill set, this candidate showed me a skill I didn't know I deeply needed on my team, and I ended up hiring her.

The Flipped Mentality

To get out of the tailored resume mindset, you need to fully connect with your L&D niche. Remember, you created that niche so you could stop trying to fit into every job description box. You should use your niche to create one resume that highlights your skills, interests, and experience.

Figure 7-1 provides a visual of these two application strategies. The image on the left shows the outdated way of applying to roles: Creating a resume for each job you want to apply for. The image on the right represents the niche-aligned way of applying to roles: Creating one resume and applying to roles that suit your career needs, interests, skills, and experience.

Figure 7-1. Outdated vs. Modern, Niche-Aligned Application Strategies

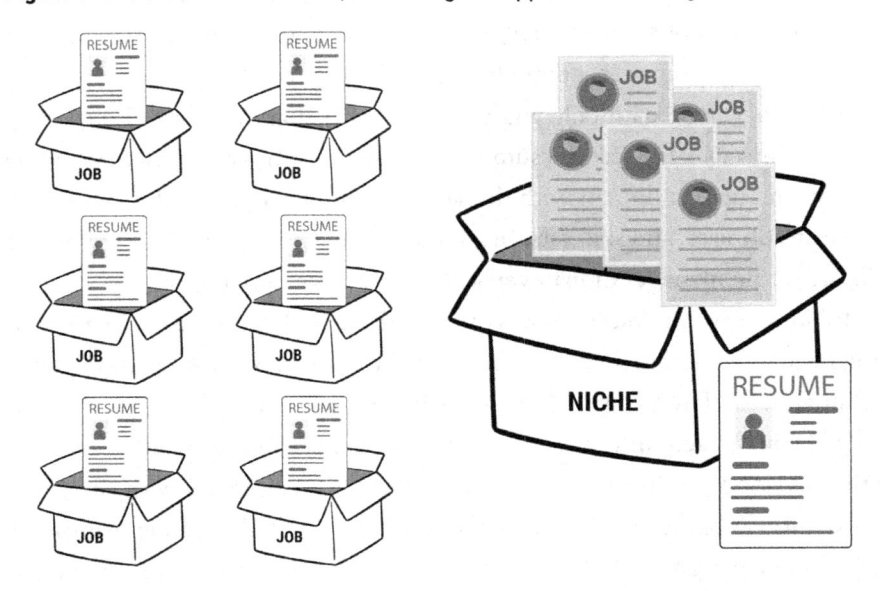

Resume Cardinal Rules

Before we start putting together your niche-aligned one-and-done resume, you must be acquainted with four cardinal resume rules thou shall not break:

1. **Not everything goes.** Your resume is a marketing document showcasing what you want to do next, through the lens of what you've done in the past. If a specific job responsibility doesn't align with the direction you want to move and you have no interest in doing, leave it off your resume. For example, I've worked with quite a few people who loathe public speaking and facilitation, yet they showcased it proudly on their resume only to be repeatedly disappointed when interviewers brought it up and asked about using it on the job.
2. **Length (kind of) doesn't matter.** In 2024, I had a client A/B test a one-page and two-page resume, and we found that the length made no difference in the percentage of callbacks she got for a first interview. As long as all your experience is relevant to your niche, and you don't exceed two pages, don't fret over the length.

3. **The ATS robots aren't out to get you (yet).** While many organizations use an applicant tracking system (ATS) to store applicant data, very few use it to scan resumes and automatically reject candidates on behalf of recruiters. You may have heard the myth that "75 percent of all resumes are rejected by the ATS." Well, that statistic was debunked in a 2020 study by HR consultant Christine Assaf who concluded that while an ATS may "weigh, or sort, or filter" your resume, it doesn't outright reject them, and "any recruiter will tell you that most if not all resumes are reviewed by a person." Write your resume with a human in mind because, for now, that's who's reading it.
4. **Function over fashion.** One of the biggest mistakes I see is people focusing on making their resume pretty rather than keeping it simple and clean. While the ATS won't automatically reject you based on your keywords or experience, if it can't translate your resume into its system, your resume may become unreadable to the recruiting team. Create your resume in Microsoft Word or Google Docs and generate a .docx and PDF version. (If you are looking for resume design inspiration, you can find ready-made Word or Google Docs templates on the creator marketplace Etsy.com. Just make sure to keep it simple.)

And here's a bonus tip: Before embarking on your resume journey, it's important to research resume norms for the country you are applying to work in. For example, many countries around the world not only embrace including a photograph of yourself on your resume, but expect it; however, in the US, this practice is frowned upon (in fact, some companies have antibias policies that remove any resume with a picture from the running).

The Five Parts of a Niche-Aligned Resume

Now that we've got the rules down, let's start creating your resume! The five parts to pay attention to are the header, profile statement, experience, education, and technology and technical skills.

1. Header

Your header must always include your first and last name, your contact information (phone number and email address), and your city and state. As a best practice, add the link to your LinkedIn profile and portfolio, if you have one.

In addition, you may choose to include a tagline that aligns with your niche to add character, personality, and alignment to your resume.

> **Meet Jeff:** When Jeff and I began working together in spring 2024, he had just begun his career search and formal transition into the L&D field. With a rich, 20-year background that spanned video game design and development, higher education, outbound sales, entrepreneurship, and sustainability, Jeff didn't quite know how to tell a cohesive story that aligned with his new career aspirations.
>
> Our first step was to home in on his niche: "Transform institutional sales and product knowledge into experiential learning programs by leveraging my analysis, problem-solving, and presentation skills for organizations that value effectiveness, continuous improvement, and creativity and want to leave the world a better place than they found it,"
>
> Jeff then decided to use "Sales Enablement Champion" as his tagline because it captured the essence of his passion:
>
> **JEFF HAYES** Sales Enablement Champion
> 310-968-1804 | findjeffhayes@gmail.com | Los Angeles, CA | linkedin.com/in/jeffreywarrenhayes | Portfolio

2. Profile Statement

Your profile statement is where a recruiter or hiring manager gets their first, brief introduction to you, your experience, and your personality. (Note: You can also call this section a career summary if that feels better to you.) If the experience section is the main attraction, I like to think of the profile statement as the movie poster that grabs the recruiter's attention and makes them want to continue reading. When creating your profile statement, be sure to cross-reference your L&D niche and incorporate that into your statement.

While there isn't a specific style you need to follow, you want to make sure your profile statement highlights three points:

1. What you do, how long you've done it, and who you've done it for.

2. The skills and strengths you've used in your career (essentially your "secret sauce").
3. Who you are, what motivates you, and how you work best.

Jeff chose to use the term career summary on his resume. Here's what he wrote:

> **CAREER SUMMARY**
> Process-oriented Sales Enablement pro with 20 years' experience growing revenues of professional services providers. Seasoned networker committed to transforming institutional knowledge and best practices into context-led learning programs. Driven to generate sustained profitable sales growth for organizations that want to leave the world in a better place.

3. Experience

Your experience section is how the person reading your resume knows whether your background aligns with their expectations of the role.

According to a recruiter eye-tracking study by Ladders, the average recruiter or hiring manager typically spends seven to eight seconds initially scanning a resume's job titles and any headings or subheadings to determine if you meet the basic qualifications for the role. However, if the resume passes this initial screening, the recruiter or hiring manager will then spend more time thoroughly reviewing it, often between 30 seconds and a few minutes. The more qualified you appear, the longer they will take to analyze the details of your experience and accomplishments.

So, if titles, headings, and subheadings are what recruiters and hiring managers look at first, you need to structure your resume so it's as easy and seamless as possible for them to find the information they need to make the decision to spend more time with your resume.

Enter the skills-chronological hybrid resume. The typical chronological resume highlights achievements from your career in a chronological order, while a skills-based resume focuses primarily on highlighting skills and providing specific examples of that skill. The problem with the chronological resume is that it's not easy to scan, so quality information can get buried inside. Similarly, skills-based resumes are typically more laborious to read and it's challenging to piece together the timeline of your work history.

The skills-chronological hybrid resume takes the best of both worlds and combines that with what we know about where recruiters' and hiring managers' eyes are tracking. To be fair, I didn't invent this type of resume (although I think I can take credit for naming it). My husband was taught a similar method as part of his graduate curriculum at Harvard Business School; once I saw his resume (and how well it worked), I knew it would lend itself well to L&D resumes.

Structuring Your Skills-Chronological Hybrid Resume

To make a skills-chronological resume that works, you'll want ask yourself the following questions for each role you've held:
- What are your proudest moments and accomplishments?
- What skills did you use to make those moments or accomplishments a reality?
- Which of those skills would you like to use in your next role? Which should you leave behind because they no longer bring you energy?

Let's revisit Jeff. As he was reviewing his work history, he listed the following as his proudest accomplishments from his most recent work experience:
- Saving a client from needing to layoff two-thirds of their workforce by increasing sales
- Evaluating sales systems and creating a new sales training program
- Coaching teams on how to implement selling techniques
- Creating and implementing a B2B sales portal to house all sales and training content
- Increasing overall client revenues by 1.5x to 3x in 6 to 12 months

The skills he used to make those accomplishments a reality included sales enablement, coaching, marketing and advertising, internal and external consulting, technology implementation, process analysis, and client prospecting.

When tasked with considering which skills he would like to use in his next role, Jeff aligned with every skill except marketing and advertising and client prospecting. While he was really good at those skills, they didn't bring him energy like the others.

Remember, your resume showcases what you want to do next, so this step is crucial in determining how you market yourself for a role that aligns with your niche.

Note: You'll notice Jeff's list of skills skews on the side of hard skills versus soft skills (such as problem solving, conflict resolution, and listening) or personality-based skills (such as creativity and work ethic). While you can include more of the softer or personality-based skills in your profile statement and cover letter (which we cover later in this chapter), the purpose of the experience section is to showcase the hard skills you use to complete on-the-job tasks.

Building Your Resume Bullet Points

Now that you have generated a skills list for each role, you need to build a high-quality bullet point aligned with each skill. Use this framework to create the three parts:

1. **What you did.** This is the tangible output and typically starts with an action verb, such as *led, developed, oversaw, created, facilitated,* or *designed.* For example, "Designed and developed instructional content for 1,200+ learners across six different programs."
2. **How you did it.** This provides brief additional context into the output. Think of it as a mini peek behind the curtains into how the tangible output came to fruition. For example, "Creating ILT, vILT, e-learning modules, facilitator and participant guides, job aids, and additional learning materials."
3. **The impact it had.** This part shows the impact, intended impact, or any additional metrics to support this skill. While it's important to try to include this for every bullet point, not every impact can be quantified (or you may not have been privy to the details of the impact). When possible, use the terms *increasing* or *decreasing* to showcase impact most effectively. "Increased overall program reach and engagement by 33 percent" is an example of an impact statement that includes a metric; "Improving strategic decision making and outcomes, increasing overall client retention" doesn't include a metric.

Once you apply the framework, combine the three parts and attach the skill to the beginning of your bullet point. It should look like this:

Instructional Design: Design and develop instructional content for 1,200+ learners by creating ILT, vILT, e-learning modules, job aids, and additional instructional materials across six learning programs, increasing overall program engagement by 33 percent.

Note: When combining your "what," "how," and "impact," make sure you finesse and streamline the sentence. It's easy to combine your statements into one long incoherent statement. Remember—how it reads is just as important as what it says.

Back to Jeff. By using this framework to highlight the skills he wanted to use in his next role, Jeff showcased to the recruiter and hiring manager the output, process, and impact he not only brought to his previous role, but what he could bring to their team and organization.

PROFESSIONAL EXPERIENCE
FOUNDER/B2B REVENUE COACH *SellWell Solutions* 2020–present
- **Sales Training and Enablement:** Deliver tailored training solutions, develop visual aids, simplify sales techniques and workflows, and provide ongoing feedback, increasing conversion rates ~53% MoM and win rates by 175%.
- **B2B Revenue Coaching:** Transform team's approach to sales through coaching and implementing state-based selling techniques, conducting gap analyses, addressing sales pipeline friction points, and guiding execution of new strategies, increasing client revenues 1.5x–3x within 6–12 months.
- **Consulting:** Facilitate partner discussions to identify underlying issues, solutions, and translate vision into actionable plans with measurable outcomes, leading to the discovery of a hidden revenue source suitable for partner buy-out.
- **Process Analysis:** Conduct detailed evaluations of sales systems, mapping out structures and functions, eliminating inefficiencies, and providing clear recommendations for improvement, increasing annual sales revenue by 2x.
- **Technology Implementation:** Developed an asynchronous B2B sales training portal with 30 lessons plus 12 hands-on labs, streamlining all content and increasing overall learning engagement and adoption.

AI Pro Tip

While I do not recommend having AI write your resume for you (because until AI can also interview for you, you still need to defend and explain your resume during an interview), it is very helpful for combining bullet points and making them more clear and concise.

Here is a sample prompt for combining like bullet points or making a long one more concise:

> Act like an expert Learning and Development resume writer, writing a resume for someone who [*insert your L&D niche*]. Here are several resume bullet points that need to be condensed into one new bullet. The new bullet point should be concise, yet clear, on what you did, how you did it, and the impact it had. Each bullet point should be structured with one headlining skill that aligns with the headlining skills already stated, followed by the description of what you did, how you did it, and the impact it had. Here is an example to follow:
>
> Succession planning: Designed a road map for talent mobility up and across the organization focusing on leadership development, product education, career coaching, and practical application, reducing turnover by 12.5% YoY.
>
> Here are the bullet points you need to condense into one new bullet:
> - [*Bullet 1*]
> - [*Bullet 2*]
> - [*Bullet 3*]
>
> When crafting your new bullet point, please make sure to remove any jargon that does not align with corporate learning and development, and focus on keeping the bullet point high level and clear. It should be as concise and succinct as possible, and no more than two sentences, although one sentence is preferable.

According to L&D and AI expert Ross Stevenson, on average, it takes eight interactions with an AI tool like ChatGPT to produce the best output, so be sure to give whatever AI tool you're using feedback and use your own human brain to make any necessary tweaks.

4. Education

When showcasing your education, relevancy is key. While you should include all formal degree programs (whether they directly align with your niche or not), be selective in sharing certifications, coursework, or programs that you won't be using in the future. For example, I have a certification in holistic health and nutrition—however, because it doesn't align with my current career goals, it's not on my resume. Be selective here. Additionally, you do not need to include your dates of graduation or program completion for any education credentials.

> Let's take a look at Jeff's education section. Note that while he does have additional coursework and certifications, none were relevant or aligned with the type of role he wanted to pursue.
>
> **EDUCATION**
> BACHELOR OF MUSIC | Film Scoring program | Berklee College of Music
> CERTIFIED IMPLEMENTOR | Global Reporting Initiative Framework 3.1 | ISOS Group-certified

5. Technology and Technical Skills

L&D and technology now go hand-in-hand, so it's expected that you'll have some technical proficiency—whether in facilitation tools like Zoom or Butter, rapid course design or video editing programs like Articulate Rise or Camtasia, or project management tools like Asana or Notion.

While each niche will encompass its own set of technology needs, use this space to highlight the tools you are familiar with and would ideally like to use (or an equivalent) in your next role. Similar to the education section, relevancy is key here.

> Let's explore Jeff's technical skills. With a background in sales, he is proficient in quite a few sales tools—all of which are relevant to his niche and future field of sales enablement. However, if Jeff had chosen a different niche, some of his more sales-focused technical skills would no longer be relevant and he would have dropped them from his resume.
>
> **TECHNICAL SKILLS**
> Canva | Pipedrive | MS Suite | Brightspace LMS | DaVinci | Slack | Google Suite | ChatGPT | Asana | Otter | Adobe Suite | LinkedIn Navigator | Hunter.io | Apollo.io | ContactScience

What About Volunteer Work, Hobbies, Interests, and Publications?

Now that we've put together your entire resume, you might be wondering if you should include volunteer work, hobbies, interests, or publications. The short answer is no, although it depends. Don't include your volunteer work or publications unless they're hyper-aligned with your niche (meaning there is a direct correlation to your niche and the roles inside of it). Hobbies and interests should remain off your professional resume.

> Jeff wrote and published a book for B2B salespeople, which would be considered hyper-aligned. So he included a publications section in his resume.
>
> **PUBLICATIONS**
> *Networking Navigator: A Playbook for B2B Networking* |
> Author | Self-published   2023
>
> "A Methodology for Creating Gameplay Animations" | Author and
> Presenter | Game Developers Conference   1998

Putting It All Together

Once you've laid out all your work experience and crafted your bullet points, you can flow them into a functional resume template. Now, you're almost ready to send it out into the world. Figure 7-2 presents a complete copy of Jeff's resume.

Final Edits

Before you cross "create a signature one-and-done resume" off your to-do list, you'll want to do a final round of edits. Here are the key things to review:

- **Check for consistency.** In the editing process, it's easy to accidentally change a font size or type of font or to insert an extra space between lines.
- **Make it scannable.** Your font size must be large enough to read—no smaller than 10pt. Your headings should be clearly indicated because that's what recruiters and hiring managers are scanning for.

Figure 7-2. Jeff's Full Resume

JEFF HAYES
Sales Enablement Champion
310-968-1804 | findjeffhayes@gmail.com | Los Angeles, CA | linkedin.com/in/jeffreywarrenhayes | Portfolio

PROFESSIONAL EXPERIENCE
FOUNDER/B2B REVENUE COACH *SellWell Solutions* — 2020–present
- **Sales Training and Enablement:** Deliver tailored training solutions, develop visual aids, simplify sales techniques and workflows, and provide ongoing feedback, increasing conversion rates ~53% MoM and win rates by 175%.
- **B2B Revenue Coaching:** Transform team's approach to sales through coaching and implementing state-based selling techniques, conducting gap analyses, addressing sales pipeline friction points, and guiding execution of new strategies, increasing client revenues 1.5x–3x within 6–12 months.
- **Consulting:** Facilitate partner discussions to identify underlying issues, solutions, and translate vision into actionable plans with measurable outcomes, leading to the discovery of a hidden revenue source suitable for partner buy-out.
- **Process Analysis:** Conduct detailed evaluations of sales systems, mapping out structures and functions, eliminating inefficiencies, and providing clear recommendations for improvement, increasing annual sales revenue by 2x.
- **Technology Implementation:** Developed an asynchronous B2B sales training portal with 30 lessons plus 12 hands-on labs, streamlining all content and increasing overall learning engagement and adoption.

ADULT EDUCATION INSTRUCTOR *Pacific Lutheran University* — 2021–2023
- **Curriculum Designer/Developer/Facilitator—B2B Sales:** Created and delivered asynchronous sales training courses for 700+ adult learners, set learning objectives (Improve Your Presentation Skills, Learn a Repeatable Selling System, Cultivate a Pipeline of Profitable Prospects, Uncover Your Authentic Sales Superpower), writing content, incorporating knowledge checks, assessments, resulting in an 87% positive course recommendation rate.

SENIOR BUSINESS DEVELOPMENT EXECUTIVE *Fusion Tek* — 2016–2020
- **Outbound Sales:** Sold IT services and support to professional services firms. Qualified leads, ran discovery, presented proposals, and closed deals while developing and maintaining talk tracks and process documents. Made >25,000 cold calls. Exceeded quota consistently. Generated >300% revenue growth over 54 months.

OPERATIONS COACH & SUSTAINABILITY COACH *The Vector Group* — 2003–2016
- **Stakeholder Engagement:** Conducted one-on-one interviews with key stakeholders to identify hidden growth opportunities and internal resistance to change. Presented summaries to improve strategic decision-making and outcomes, increasing overall client productivity and profitability.
- **Global Reporting:** Led team of 200 to produce annual environmental report conforming to international standards. Defined scope, determined materiality, collected and analyzed raw data, and designed layout, improving brand perception.
- **Data Visualization:** Led the design and development of a cutting-edge application for visualizing data by formulating algorithms into 3D representations. Oversaw a cross-functional team and brought needs-aligned solution to market.

ANIMATION DIRECTOR/ANIMATOR *Various, including Walt Disney Imagineering, Activision, Metrolight* — 1992–2003
- **Leadership:** Directed cross-functional content teams by delegating responsibilities, providing feedback, ensuring accountability, and aligning individual efforts with strategic objectives, increasing output and productivity by 50%.
- **Digital/Virtual Asset Development:** Created animations for virtual reality, video games, and visual effects studios, overseeing asset deployment and establishing prodction pipelines. Product releases generated >$350M in revenue.

TECHNICAL SKILLS
Canva | Pipedrive | MS Suite | Brightspace LMS | DaVinci | Slack | Google Suite | ChatGPT | Asana | Otter | Adobe Suite | LinkedIn Navigator | Hunter.io | Apollo.io | ContactScience

EDUCATION
BACHELOR OF MUSIC | Film Scoring program | Berklee College of Music
CERTIFIED IMPLEMENTOR | Global Reporting Initiative Framework 3.1 | ISOS Group-certified

PUBLICATIONS
Networking Navigator: A Playbook for B2B Networking | Author | Self-published — 2023
"A Methodology for Creating Gameplay Animations" | Author/Presenter | Game Developers Conference — 1998

- **Follow the $100 rule.** I typically encourage my clients to take two to three additional passes at their resume using the $100 rule: If you had to pay $100 for each word on your resume, what stays and what goes? It's a great way to edit down any wordy parts.

And voila! You now have a niche-aligned resume. Make sure to revisit chapter 4 to ensure you've got a strong strategy ready for applying to niche-aligned roles.

Note: While this is the most recommended framework for converting applications to interviews, there are many ways this format can manifest. The resources link at the end of this book provides more resume samples for you to review.

Your New Cover Letter Template

I know, I know. It's time to write the dreaded cover letter. You may even be asking if it's even necessary. While the answer can vary depending on the employer, I always recommend including one, even if it's optional, because hiring managers are not mind-readers (yet) and a cover letter can help you stand out from the crowd. Especially in competitive job markets, a compelling cover letter may inspire a hiring manager or recruiter to dive deeper into your resume. (Note, however, that more and more employers aren't including a place to submit a cover letter—in those cases, you're off the hook.)

Just like the myth and poor advice of having to update your resume for every job application, many also believe they need to write a brand-new cover letter each time. This time consuming and unnecessary task was one of the most dreaded parts of the job application process—until now.

Your Cover Letter Is a Trailer

How often do go to a movie without watching the trailer? In our house, my husband plays the trailers for a bunch of different movies and then we decide which movie to watch based on the one that intrigues us the most.

The same can be said for cover letters—your cover letter is the trailer to your resume. It gives the recruiter or hiring manager a preview into what they can expect when they dive into your experience, while also a glimpse into your personality, strengths, and motivators. Just like a great movie trailer, a captivating cover letter creates excitement and buzz.

The best movie trailers follow a three-story act, which introduces the main character (act 1), highlights the challenge or conflict (act 2), provides a sneak peek at the climax (act 3), and ends with a call to action to watch the film. Your cover letter should follow the same format.

Act 1. Introduce the Main Character

It's time to bring your main character to center stage. The first paragraph of your cover letter showcases who you are, what you want to do, the values you wish to share with your next organization, and what drew you to the role. Use your L&D niche statement to write the opening paragraph of your cover letter.

> Jeff was now ready to create his cover letter template. He used his L&D niche statement—"I design and implement organizational transformation projects by leveraging strategic planning, program design, and leadership skills for organizations that value creativity and innovation"—to create the following introduction paragraph for his cover letter:
>
> As an experienced learning and development leader who designs and implements organizational transformation projects [niche what] and values creativity and innovation [niche who], I was immediately intrigued by the opportunity to leverage my strategic planning, program design, and leadership [niche how] skills as the next learning experience manager [job title] at Global Electric [company name].

Act 2. Highlight the Challenges

Now that the reader knows who you are, they want to know about any organizational challenges you've overcome in your career. Sharing challenges may sound counterintuitive at first, but it not only showcases what you're capable of overcoming, it allows the reader to empathize with you and invest deeper in your story. Note, however, that this is not the place to highlight personal challenges or poor working environments. Use this space to consider what you've had to face to be successful.

> Jeff decided to highlight his experience in redeveloping outdated programs and processes and scaling them with limited resources because he was proud of how he'd overcome that challenge:
>
>> Over the years, I have worked on numerous projects and programs to design and develop innovative learning experiences that are both effective and engaging. With the rapid pace of technological advancements, at many points in my L&D career, I was faced with overcoming outdated organizational processes, poor adoption of digital learning, and scaling learning programs faster than ever before to align with rapid organizational growth [challenges].

The goal is for the person reading your cover letter to look at this section and say, "Yeah—me too!"

Act 3. Sneak Peek of the Climax

Every movie has a climax—the highest point of the film when the protagonist determines what action they need to take to resolve the conflict. In your cover letter, your third paragraph shares how you took action to overcome the challenges and provides a sneak peek at your greatest accomplishments (your unforgettable scenes).

> Jeff's third paragraph outlined how he faced the challenge head on, as well as a few of his favorite accomplishments from his resume:
>
>> To overcome those organizational and learning challenges, I've leveraged my skills in process improvement, technology sourcing, facilitation, and project management [skills]. Additionally, I've focused on developing a keen eye for detail, an ability to work collaboratively, and a deep understanding of learning engagement and adoption best practices to proactively develop top-tier, highly adopted learning experiences [skills].
>>
>> Some highlights from my experience that align with what this role is looking to achieve include:
>> - Designing and developing 25+ courses and programs, resulting in a 200% enrollment growth within 5 years [achievement from resume]
>> - Leading a collaborative cross-functional team of external contractors and designers to produce 10 large-scale learning projects annually on fast timelines and with tight budgets [achievement from resume]

- Researching and incorporating learning technologies, including selecting and implementing a new LMS and training super-users, increasing overall digital content adoption to 97% [achievement from resume]

Call to Action

Like every movie trailer has a call to action (CTA) to watch the movie, your cover letter's call to action is to get the reader to review your resume.

> Jeff kept his CTA short, simple, and to the point:
>
> My resume details my specific skills and experiences most aligned with this role. I appreciate your consideration and look forward to discussing how I can add value to Global Electric [company name] in this capacity.

When you follow this format, the only information you have to update or tailor for each role is the position title in act 1 and the company name in acts 1 and 3. If you have some additional time and want to tailor even more, you can swap out the achievements listed in act 2 to other line items from your resume.

What's Next? Get Ready to Write!

Your resume and cover letter are by far the heaviest lifts of the entire career transition and job seeking process. Once you complete your one-and-done resume, use it to write your niche-aligned cover letter, and focus on applying to roles aligned with your skills, interests, and values, however, you will find that the time it takes for you to apply to roles will be cut by as much as 90 percent. Here are a few things to remember as you create your resume and cover letter:

- Structure your resume using the skills-chronological hybrid format, emphasizing key skills and accomplishments. Bonus: Apply the $100 rule to make your resume more concise.
- Design a cover letter template that follows the three-act structure: Introduce yourself, highlight challenges you've overcome, and showcase your key accomplishments. Remember, this is the trailer to your resume—make it compelling!

Chapter 8
Building Your L&D Personal Brand

"Personal branding is not about being perfect. It's about being yourself, and showcasing your unique talents and skills to the world." —Christina Lattimer

When you think about the word *personal brand*, what comes to mind? Do you think about building a website? Shameless self-promotion or thought leadership? Having to become an influencer or content creator?

Personal branding has gotten a bad rap over the years, with many people believing they have to hustle to manufacture a persona for the outside world; however, that couldn't be further from the truth. According to personal branding expert William Arruda (2024), "Authenticity is the cornerstone of personal branding. It's about discovering what's true, genuine, and real about you and presenting that to the world. Although the digital world has made it easier to build a brand, building a brand around a manufactured image may not be impactful in the long run."

An authentic personal brand has many benefits, and, when it comes to investing time into your own career transformation, it allows you to expand your network by connecting with like-minded L&D practitioners, increase your credibility, and make you stand out to potential employers—especially in a competitive market.

The important thing to keep in mind, however, is that having a personal brand requires you to have a presence. The thought of creating a personal brand from scratch or growing one you already have may seem intimidating but, remember, personal branding is personal. Your brand exists on a spectrum and you do not need to have an advanced personal brand to be successful in your L&D career.

So, while you may feel like you need to become a full-blown content creator to have a personal brand, know that you have many other options to choose from that range from passive to active involvement (Figure 8-1).

Figure 8-1. The Personal Brand Spectrum: From Passive to Active

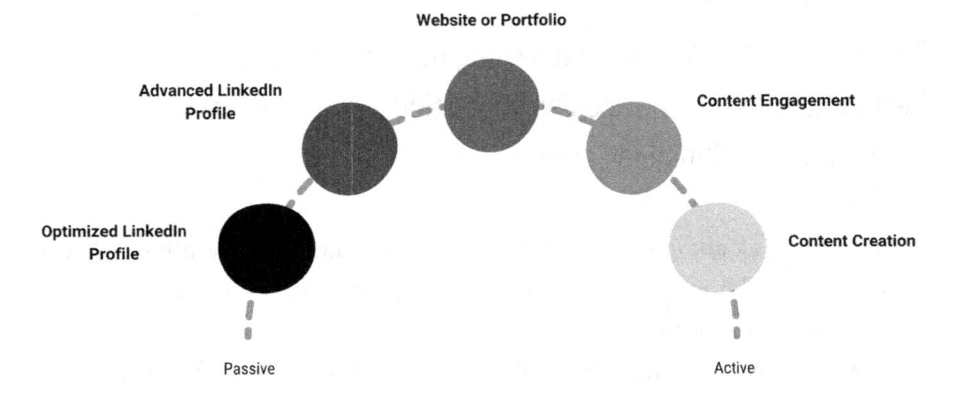

> **Activity**
> Take a few moments to identify where you are on the personal brand spectrum, and where you might like to be.

Getting Started

Every well-known brand has a set of brand goals and pillars. Apple's goals of being known for sleek product designs, intuitive interfaces, and emphasis on user privacy align directly with their brand pillars of innovation, simplicity, design, user experience, and privacy and security. Amazon's brand pillars of customer obsession, innovation, convenience, selection, and value are evident in their goal to be known for vast product selection, fast shipping options, and having a customer-centric approach.

Brand pillars make the process of developing a cohesive personal brand way more effective (and manageable) by giving you a structure to follow and ensuring your brand message aligns not only with who you are, but what you want to be known for. Because your personal brand is so unique to you, it's important to calibrate your own set of personal brand goals and pillars before you start creating or growing it.

Goals and Aspirations

The first step is to set your direction. When thinking about your personal brand, do you want to establish yourself as a thought leader, attract a new job opportunity, inspire change around a specific idea, or learn from and engage with your peers? You can have more than one goal, but as you continue building your brand, you'll want to come back to them often to assess if your brand is getting you closer to your goals and aspirations.

Pillar 1. Impact

To use your personal brand to grow in your L&D career, you want it to reflect the impact you're looking to make. For this pillar, spend time reflecting on any specific improvements you want to contribute to your next company and what lasting impression you'd like to leave in your next role.

Pillar 2. Skills and Interests

Your personal brand should showcase your skills, expertise, and interests. Consider what skills you want to be known for, what unique experiences you might have, and what you want people to say about your skills and expertise when you're not in the room.

Pillar 3. Core Values

Your core values are the backbone of your brand—they influence the way you work and interact with others. Reflect on what values and foundational beliefs guide your decision making and how you want your personal values to align with the culture of your next company.

> **Activity**
> Before going any further in bringing your personal brand to life, reflect on your personal brand goals and aspirations, as well as the three personal brand pillars.

The Personal Brand Spectrum

Now that your goals are established and your pillars are in place, let's explore each piece of the personal brand spectrum.

> **Meet Piri:** In 2021, Piri transitioned from K–12 education into a successful freelance career in instructional design. By late 2023, she was ready to land her dream in-house L&D role—except her personal brand didn't reflect these new goals. When we reviewed the story her brand was telling, she realized it was stuck in limbo between her careers in K–12 and as a freelancer. It wasn't closely tied to her brand pillars or what she wanted to do in her next role. So, we started off by polishing up her LinkedIn profile.

Basic LinkedIn Profile

At the very minimum, your personal brand should feature a completed LinkedIn profile. According to Jobscan, 87 percent of recruiters use LinkedIn to source candidates (Purcell 2024). In addition, six people are hired through LinkedIn every minute! Let's look closer at the eight components of a basic profile.

Profile Picture

Profiles that include a good quality photo receive 21 times more profile views than those that don't—so this is an easy way to get more eyes on your profile (Callahan 2018). Make sure your photo is high resolution, recent, just of you, and has a plain background. You also want to ensure it's not too zoomed in or out.

Banner

Think of your banner (the rectangle image at the very top of your profile) as your billboard. It should represent you and any (or all) of your brand pillars.

> Piri's first step was refreshing her LinkedIn banner. She decided to include a photo of herself and a statement representing her brand pillars: "to build learning programs and solve business problems."

Headline

Your headline is your value proposition statement and one of the most searchable parts of your profile. It not only helps optimize your profile, but tells a quick story about what you can bring to the table so future employers won't have to click through your entire profile. (Your headline is a great place to include an abridged version of your niche statement from chapter 4.) You also want to include two to three of the aligned job titles you wrote in the outside rim of your career golden circle.

> Piri's LinkedIn headline stated that she wanted to "analyze, design, and develop streamlined learning programs for innovative organizations." Then, she listed out a few of the jobs in her career golden circle, including instructional designer, learning and development specialist, and e-developer.

About

The about section is not the time to highlight your specific experience—that's what the experience section is for. Use this part of your LinkedIn profile to tell the story of why you do what you do, who you are, and what you can do for a future employer.

> Here's how Piri told her "why" story:

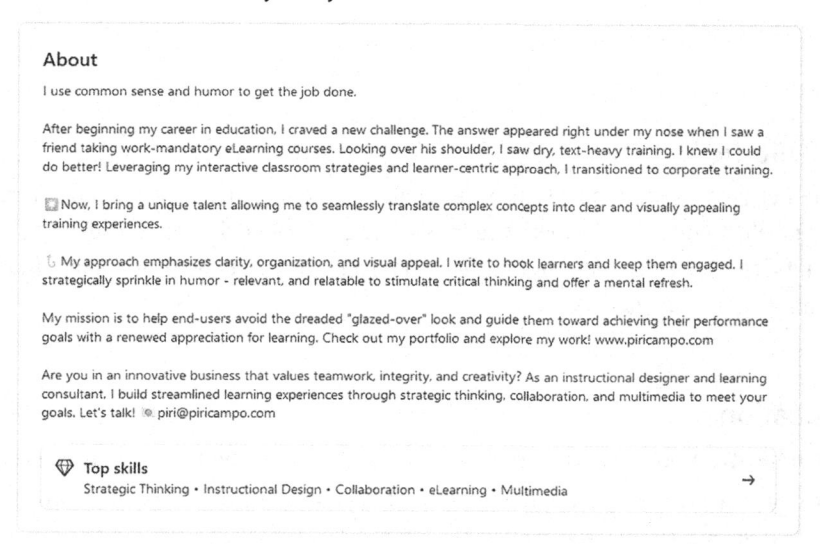

About

I use common sense and humor to get the job done.

After beginning my career in education, I craved a new challenge. The answer appeared right under my nose when I saw a friend taking work-mandatory eLearning courses. Looking over his shoulder, I saw dry, text-heavy training. I knew I could do better! Leveraging my interactive classroom strategies and learner-centric approach, I transitioned to corporate training.

Now, I bring a unique talent allowing me to seamlessly translate complex concepts into clear and visually appealing training experiences.

My approach emphasizes clarity, organization, and visual appeal. I write to hook learners and keep them engaged. I strategically sprinkle in humor - relevant, and relatable to stimulate critical thinking and offer a mental refresh.

My mission is to help end-users avoid the dreaded "glazed-over" look and guide them toward achieving their performance goals with a renewed appreciation for learning. Check out my portfolio and explore my work! www.piricampo.com

Are you in an innovative business that values teamwork, integrity, and creativity? As an instructional designer and learning consultant, I build streamlined learning experiences through strategic thinking, collaboration, and multimedia to meet your goals. Let's talk! piri@piricampo.com

Top skills
Strategic Thinking • Instructional Design • Collaboration • eLearning • Multimedia

Experience

Your experience should focus on the most relevant examples that align with the type of roles you want—don't include a laundry list of everything you've ever done. Be sure to highlight the skills, interests, expertise you outlined in your brand pillars.

> In her experience section, Piri heavily featured her roles as an instructional designer, e-developer, and learning and development consultant.
>
> **Experience**
>
> **Instructional Designer | eDeveloper | Learning & Development Consultant**
> Piri Campo · Self-employed
> Nov 2021 - Present · 3 yrs 3 mos
> Houston, Texas, United States · Hybrid
>
> - Migrated instructional content from Lessonly to Articulate Rise, incorporated edits based on internal quality assurance reviews, and completed courses according to schedule.
>
> - Reduced New Hire Turnover: Developed an onboarding and training program for 200+ new employees, resulting in decreased turnover.
>
> - Increased Safety Training Retention by 15%: Used Action Mapping to identify skill and knowledge gaps in a safety training program, leading to a retention boost.
>
> - Developed Engaging Multimedia Learning: Designed training using various multimedia elements (instructor-led, blended, eLearning, hybrid) to close knowledge and skills gaps.
>
> - Created Compelling Video Content: Scripted and directed 10 high-resolution video captures and 4 video demonstrations for safety and training procedures, exceeding EH&S and DOT standards.
>
> - Designed Effective Curriculum: Developed learning objectives and experiences to prioritize behavioral changes to avoid revenue loss from remediation.
>
> ♢ Project Management, Instructional Videos and +20 skills

AI Pro Tip

Rather than listing a bunch of bullet points, you may opt to write a short blurb highlighting the overall experience for each role you've held. If you decide to go in that direction, an AI tool like ChatGPT can help synthesize the bullet points from your resume into your blurb.

Education

The education section is a prime location to list your degrees and any relevant certifications, trainings, coursework, and licenses. Similar to your resume, you don't need to include graduation dates for your degrees.

Piri's education section features her bachelor's and master's degrees, as well as any applicable certifications and credentials. While Piri has other certifications and licenses from her time in the K–12 space, she opted to remove them because they're not relevant to her current job search.

Education

Truman State University
Master of Arts in Education
◇ Articulate Rise

Truman State University
Bachelor of English

Licenses & certifications

Developing Your Emotional Intelligence
LinkedIn
Issued Nov 2024
(Show credential ↗)
◇ Emotional Intelligence

TechSmith Camtasia 2022 Explorer
TechSmith
Issued Feb 2023 · Expires Feb 2025
Credential ID nnvdixu5pdin
(Show credential ↗)

Skills

When recruiters are looking for candidates, one of the criteria they look for are skills. This section should feature skills that align with the type of roles you are pursuing (or your niche).

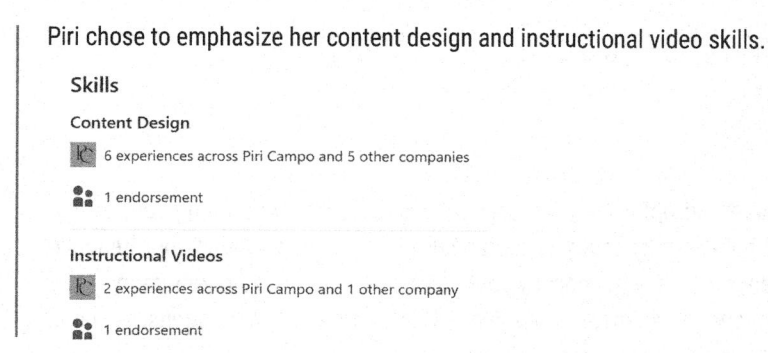

Piri chose to emphasize her content design and instructional video skills.

Skills

Content Design
6 experiences across Piri Campo and 5 other companies
1 endorsement

Instructional Videos
2 experiences across Piri Campo and 1 other company
1 endorsement

Recommendations

Think of the recommendations section as you would a testimonial on a website—social proof of your personal brand. You want to aim for at least three recent recommendations. If you ask someone to write a recommendation for you, share a bit about your personal brand and the types of roles you're targeting so they can cater their recommendation accordingly.

Piri got a testimonial from a former teammate on an onboarding project and displayed it in her profile.

Received | Given

Beth Hattier, Ed.D · 2nd
Director, Learning & Development @ Mansfield Energy Corp | EdD, Development Coach
October 26, 2023, Beth worked with Piri on the same team

I'm pleased to recommend Piri Campo for any role that involves instructional and eLearning design. I had the pleasure of working with Piri on a project aimed at onboarding new employees to our organization. From the project's inception, Piri was the instructional and eLearning designer, and she quickly showed her expertise in the field by collaborating with the team and learning the technical aspects of the business. Piri's designer and consultant skills were invaluable in navigating the stakeholders, staying curious, and focusing on the learner experience to achieve project goals. She took the time to research and understand the target audience, which helped her develop informative and relevant content. I was impressed by her willingness to collaborate and eagerness to take constructive feedback to fine-tune the learning content. Her passion for her work was evident, and it was a pleasure to work with her. Overall, Piri is a very skilled and dedicated professional who brings creativity and a learner-focused approach to all of her projects. I feel fortunate to have had the opportunity to work with her and recommend her for any role that involves instructional and eLearning design.

Veronique Frizzell · 3rd
MBA in Finance, VBA Excel, Data Analytics | Senior Financial Analyst, Controller | Exploring AI
January 9, 2023, Veronique was Piri's client

I've been on the receiving end of her training sessions, so I can speak to her capability to express materials in a clear and lucid manner. She didn't just list a series of steps but elaborated on the why of doing such steps. Doing so provided a deeper understanding of her approach. Included in her instructions were well-designed teaching materials and well-chosen examples to illustrate her thoughts. And all of this was done remotely, over Zoom. Perfect for this remote age.

She has good telegenic presence so if one needs instructional courses over Zoom, she would be a natural. Her professionalism and pleasant demeanor and soothing voice contributed to the pleasant experience.

As a matter of fact, her presentation was such a winner, the group asked her to come back and teach another topic. If that is not a resounding recommendation, I don't know what is.

Activity

Fully complete and optimize your LinkedIn profile. Start by updating your profile picture and banner to reflect your personal brand, and then refine your headline and about section to clearly convey your value proposition and career story. Last, make sure your experience, education, skills, and recommendations sections align with the roles you are targeting.

Pro tip: Start with a blank Word or Google document to brainstorm, and copy and paste your final edits into your LinkedIn profile.

Advanced LinkedIn Functions

A great way to showcase your brand-aligned work samples, articles, content, and posts is through your LinkedIn profile's featured section. Here, you can add hyperlinks, media files, PDFs, and videos, as well as pin any of your original LinkedIn posts.

According to peakprofiles.com, this section of your profile serves as "your living portfolio. You should be updating it periodically. Keep the content fresh, relevant, and engaging to users. Add a variety of content—blog posts, programs you have led or worked on, articles about your company, vertical market segment, or area of specialization."

> Shortly after aligning her LinkedIn profile with her career goals and aspirations, Piri started to receive messages from recruiters about opportunities! To keep this momentum going, she began leveraging the featured section of her LinkedIn profile.
>
> Piri used the featured section of her LinkedIn profile to link her portfolio and pin two posts about her programs—one highlighting a program's completion and the other showcasing her analysis skills.

Activity
Collect your best work samples, articles, blog posts, and any relevant media files (such as PDFs and videos) that align with your personal brand and add them to the featured section of your LinkedIn profile.

Portfolio and Work Samples

When it comes to creating a personal brand online, one of the top questions I get asked across all L&D fields, functions, and roles is "Do I need a portfolio?"

What comes to mind when you think of a traditional L&D portfolio? Do you, like many other L&D practitioners, assume it means a fully built out website, complete with navigation, asset hosting, and custom design?

In fact, "portfolios can come in all shapes and sizes," Luke Hobson writes in "So You Want to Become an Instructional Designer" (2023). "If you have your own website, that's great. If you put everything in a Google Drive folder and share it with your interviewers, that's great too." Hobson also recommends another alternative—to record a "walkthrough of your projects to highlight not only your designs, but your communication skills as well." As an example, I used the inexpensive, user-friendly portfolio site Carrd.co to create my portfolio (sarahloveslearning.carrd.co).

With that being said—do you even need a portfolio? The short answer is yes. I recommend that everyone has work samples handy (such as storyboard documentation, e-learning modules, strategy documents, training decks and materials, and so on). For roles centered around strategy, facilitation, and administration, a body of work isn't always required, but it's still helpful to have some samples to refer to. If your niche is centered on the physical design and development of learning assets, materials, and programs, however, you definitely need an easily accessible portfolio that aligns with your personal brand and showcases your design capabilities.

Whether you create a website, store your assets in a cloud-based drive, or have a recorded portfolio (or some combination of the three), you'll want to make sure your portfolio:

- **Aligns with your brand pillars.** Be selective about which samples you develop and include. For example, if your personal brand is centered around leadership development, but none of your samples align with that, your portfolio isn't telling the story of your brand.
- **Uses what you've got.** Some of my client's most successful portfolios have included YouTube videos of their facilitation, sample articles they've written, and even pictures of a whiteboard showing how a learning strategy was made. You don't have to recreate the wheel.
- **Gives context.** Hobson says the biggest mistake people make with their portfolios "is not telling enough of the story behind the projects." He suggests including a summary of the project (including the problem or goal), objectives, stakeholders, audience, and tools, in addition to the design and deliverables.

> **Activity**
> Develop or update your L&D portfolio to support your personal brand, whether through a website, cloud-based drive, or recorded walkthrough. Ensure it includes a variety of work samples with clear context and aligns with your brand pillars.

Content Engagement

Creating a personal brand does not require you to become a content creator, but this common misconception is why many people shy away from the idea. In fact, a great strategy to getting more people to visit and find your profile is by engaging with other people's content.

It's important to revisit your personal brand goals before developing your engagement strategy. "Your personal brand goal determines who your target audience is," explains Janel Abrahami, personal brand expert, L&D practitioner, and career coach. "Once you determine your target audience, you can then identify where they are in terms of what platform they are on." This allows you to actively engage with your target audience. She offers this example:

- What is your goal? Land a new full-time job ASAP.
- Who is your target audience? Recruiters and hiring managers.
- Where is your audience looking? Most likely LinkedIn.

You likely have several goals and aspirations for your personal brand, so it's OK to have several target audiences too. For example, if one of your goals is to grow your expertise in leadership development, your target audience may be leadership development practitioners and consultants. What if they are more active on TikTok than LinkedIn? Don't get stuck in a box with one target audience or specific platform.

When you engage with someone's content, it introduces the author to you and your personal brand. In addition, commenting and engaging with other creators on nearly all social platforms will boost your profile so it's easier for people to find you. However, engaging in your target audience's content is more than just smashing the like or subscribe button—it's about leaving a meaningful comment or engaging in dialogue. Let's look closer at several different types of engagement.

Validate

When you validate the author's content, you provide support for their idea through your own example or experience.

> Piri's LinkedIn connection, Matt, posted about the importance of piloting a course versus launching a perfect course, and Piri shared her support and admiration:
>
>> It's exciting that your organization understands the value of user feedback in iteration. Finding misunderstandings or gaps in the learning experiences from the user's perspective can be different than the designer or developer's perspective.

Elaborate

Elaborating on the author's content means your comment adds on to their thoughts.

> Piri left this comment on a LinkedIn post one of her connections shared about different pretraining measures that L&D folks should implement. She also shared her experience using similar measures:
>
>> I agree with you that vocabulary is essential for learning. I also like to include a glossary that references where the learner can find the vocabulary in use.

Debate

Debating (kindly and respectfully) means your comment offers a different perspective from what is presented in the original post.

> When one of Piri's LinkedIn connections shared an experiment they conducted using AI-generated voiceovers, Piri shared her dissenting perspective on the topic while engaging in dialogue with the original poster:
>
>> Are you pleased with the end results? I prefer voice actors. AI narration doesn't draw me in.

Ask

Asking the post's author a specific question can encourage further dialogue.

On a LinkedIn post about writing test questions and assessments, Piri was intrigued by the author's perspective on what they called "trash" questions:

> Excellent specifics here, Rick. It sounds like IADLEST has been around for a while. I'm curious—do they track and have data for the assessments? Is this how you compiled your specifics? Or is it mainly through experience? Over time, I use most of these. However, I'm not familiar with the why behind the "trash" options. I was wondering if you would elaborate on those. Many thanks in advance!

> **Activity**
> Identify your personal brand goals and target audiences, and then actively engage with their content on relevant platforms. Leave meaningful comments, share your experiences, and ask questions to foster dialogue and boost your profile's visibility.

Content Creation

I said it earlier and I'll say it again—you do not have to create content to have a personal brand or land your dream L&D role. However, many L&D practitioners want to share the educational content they create throughout their careers.

There are many benefits of sharing content you've created if you're an L&D job seeker. It allows you to:
- Showcase your expertise and position yourself as a thought leader.
- Broaden your reach among hiring managers, recruiters, and other L&D practitioners.
- Show off your content creation skills and demonstrate your ability to design.
- Gain feedback on your ideas and methods, which you can use to refine your approach.

Most people get stuck trying to figure out what to post. Career coach and founder of Pivot With Purpose Janel Abrahami suggests using the following structure to come up with ongoing content based on your brand pillars:
- **Here's what I know.** What can you share about your skills, interests, and experience?

- **Here's what I think.** What perspective can you add to a topic that people are already discussing?
- **Here's what I'm doing or have done.** What moment of time can you capture to share more behind-the-scenes information about a project, program, or deliverable you're working on or have worked on in the past?

Piri was determined to keep her personal brand as active as she could manage and felt called to create content. She leveraged Abrahami's structure to help her determine what kind of content to generate.

1. Here's What I Know

Piri crafted a post on LinkedIn demonstrating her expertise in creating and developing effective safety training. She finished that post with a call to action to further the dialogue around measurement and an image with the text "Congratulations, you passed!"

> **Piri Campo, M.A.E.** · 1st
> Analyze, design, and evaluate streamlined learning programs for innovati...
> 4mo ·
>
> Transitioning from educator to instructional designer was an intriguing pivot, but the biggest surprise? Passing scores in safety-first fields like construction and energy. Stakeholders often require 100% mastery, which makes perfect sense. In those industries, keeping those skills and knowledge sharp is essential.
>
> Fellow instructional designers, what is typically the passing score to guarantee learners have nailed the skills and knowledge crucial for your industry?
>
> I'm curious to hear about your experiences! Please drop a note in the comments.
>
> Congratulations, you passed!
>
> End

2. Here's What I Think

After completing an interview project, Piri shared her experience condensing a topic into a five-minute lesson. She not only related a common topic to her own experience, but she also posed a question to invite others to weigh in as well:

> **Piri Campo, M.A.E.** · 1st
> Analyze, design, and evaluate streamlined learning programs for innovati...
> 3w · 🌐
>
> Have you ever tried to condense your passion into a 5-minute lesson? It's tougher than it sounds!
>
> As part of a recent job interview process, I was tasked with creating a microlearning experience on a topic I'm both passionate and knowledgeable about. As a self-confessed foodie, food was the first subject that came to mind!
>
> This challenge opened my eyes to the Subject Matter Expert's (SME) perspective in a new way. I was brimming with ideas, which made it tough to initially zero in on the learning objective.
>
> So, I went back to the basics. I reviewed the design challenge parameters, crafted a couple of objectives, and gathered input from people across generations—both inside and outside of L&D. Their feedback, combined with Gagne's 9 Events of Learning, my development tools, and my love for cooking, helped me refine the objective. From there, the scriptwriting and storyboarding fell into place.
>
> The hardest part? Trimming the content to fit the 5-7 minute requirement. I found myself continually going back to the learning objective and storyboard to decide what to cut.
>
> My takeaways? Continue to:
>
> -Host crucial conversations between the SMEs and stakeholders early in the process.
> -Partner with SMEs and use the learning objectives to guide the process and keep the project on track without dampening their enthusiasm.
>
> How do you balance the SME's passion with precision in your projects? I'd love to hear your thoughts!

3. Here's What I'm Doing or Have Done

Piri took a minute to share an update on an onboarding program she created. She made sure to include some anecdotes from the program as well as how it's exceeding expectations:

> **Piri Campo, M.A.E.** · 1st
> Analyze, design, and develop streamlined lear...
> 2h
>
> Thrilled to see my client's new onboarding & training program exceeding expectations! 6 months ago the program launched. They achieved a remarkable 0% safety incident rate, exceeding their initial goal of 5%. The stakeholders bought into the program and the methods we developed and that was crucial.
>
> Additionally, the new hires shared their appreciation for:
>
> 🎒 The program's streamlined process, allowing them to progress quickly.
>
> 🗂 The program's clear structure ensured new hires grasped company expectations from the get-go, fostering a smooth transition.
>
> ↗ The cherry on top? Even seasoned professionals valued the program! The experienced hires found it a valuable refresher, proving a well-designed program benefits everyone.

Activity

Leverage your expertise by creating content that aligns with your personal brand pillars. Use the structure of sharing what you know, what you think, and what you're doing to showcase your skills and experience. Keep your content authentic to effectively position yourself as a thought leader and broaden your reach within the L&D community.

What's Next? Leveraging Your Personal Brand

While there are many ways to approach your personal brand, the most important thing to remember is to keep it authentic. It's easy to feel pressured to copy a specific format or style or align with whatever's new and trendy, but at the end of the day, authenticity is what fuels your personal brand. Remember, you are the only "you." Your personal brand is just that—personal.

- Reflect on your personal brand goals and pillars, considering your desired influence, skills, interests, and core values.
- Determine if you'd like your personal brand to be passive or more active (there is no wrong answer).
- Complete or update your LinkedIn profile with a high-quality photo, a banner image, a headline that reflects your niche, engaging about and education sections, and relevant skills and recommendations.
- Bonus: Engage with relevant content by commenting, elaborating, and asking questions. If inclined, create content aligned with your brand pillars using the here's what I know, here's what I think, and here's what I'm doing or have done structure.

PART 3
Networking and Building Relationships

Chapter 9
The 3 Ls of Networking

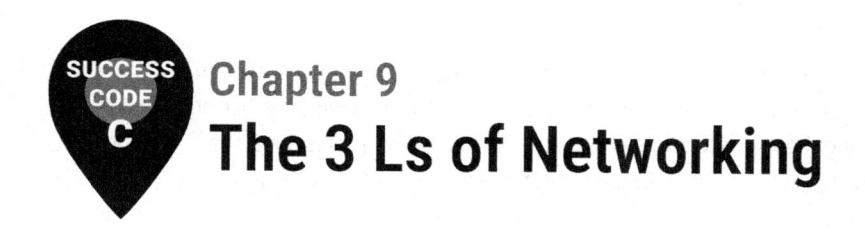

"Networking is not about just connecting people. It's about connecting people with people, people with ideas, and people with opportunities." —Michele Jennae

When you think about networking, what is the first thought or feeling that comes to mind? Maybe you feel excited and intrigued? Or do you feel overwhelmed and phony? Regardless of how you feel about the idea of networking, the research can't be ignored. Researchers at Harvard University studied a group of more than 165 lawyers and found that their "success depended on their ability to network effectively both internally (to get themselves assigned to choice clients) and externally (to bring business into the firm). Those who regarded these activities as distasteful and avoided them had fewer billable hours than their peers" (Gino, Kouchaki, and Casciaro 2016). To reach your ultimate career goals, you'll almost undoubtedly need to network or rely on those in your network.

Here's the good news. Over the past several years, the way we network has dramatically shifted. What was once a world of in-person events where you handed out your business card and left with a giant stack of new ones, has now become even more accessible and authentic than ever before due to digital networking. While we once only networked with peers in our local area, we are now networking around the globe, often from the comfort of our own homes.

Whether you've always loved to network, have grown to tolerate it, or still struggle with making it a priority, there's one important thing to remember: Networking will always pay off; it's just out of our control as to when.

Meet Brittany E. As a new instructional designer in the government sector, Brittany had to hit the ground running and with little guidance or training from her organization. So, she sought out a networking group of other newer L&D professionals to learn from. She also met a peer, Lisa, in this group and they grew a professional relationship. About a year later, after revisiting her L&D niche, Brittany began exploring project management opportunities. Turns out, Lisa's organization had an opening for an L&D project manager role! Lisa referred Brittany to the role and a few weeks later, she'd landed the job. When Brittany met Lisa, she didn't focus on when or how—or even if—it would pay off, but it surely did.

Brittany's story is not an isolated incident. In fact, 80 percent of professionals find networking essential to their career success and 41 percent want to network more often (Bradshaw 2024). You, too, can learn to love networking.

Now that networking is more accessible than ever, it's also equally important to note that quality will always win over quantity. Here's what to avoid:

- **Collecting LinkedIn connections.** Many people put too much emphasis on how many followers or connections they have on LinkedIn, without putting conscious thought into the quality of these connections. Having 500 apples doesn't help me if I need an orange, and the same thing goes for the number of LinkedIn connections I have (or the number of connections I have in general).
- **Joining every networking group, event, and program.** Networking only works when you're intentional about it. If you overextend yourself, you won't be able to dedicate time to building intentional connections inside these groups.
- **An opportunity to only take.** The biggest misconception about networking is that we should only focus on what we can get out of it. While we all hope to be able to lean on our network in one way or another (now or in the future), we can't forget that it's a two-way street. If your idea of networking is constantly asking people to help you, then you need to realize that you're actually just seeking advice, not networking.

To network authentically, you will need to focus on three steps:

1. **Set your networking goals.** You can't create an aligned network if you don't know what you're aligning toward.

2. **Perfect your elevator pitch.** It's important you're clear on who you are, what you offer, and what you want to learn from networking—and that you can articulate that.
3. **Build your L&D networking ecosystem.** Variety is key, so diversify where and how you network.

Setting Your Networking Goals

How many times have you come across someone in your network and wondered how they got there, where you first met them, and why you'd ever be connected to them? If you've wracked your brain and still don't have an answer, they're probably not aligned with your networking goals.

I may be dating myself, but I've seen many clients come to me after approaching their networking journey like *Supermarket Sweep*. For those of you unfamiliar with this '90s show, here's the premise: Contestants raced through a grocery store and "swept" groceries into their cart. Whoever had the most groceries when the time ran out won. Sound like your networking journey? How often have you felt the need to "sweep" as many LinkedIn connections into your proverbial basket as possible, without really asking yourself whether they were aligned with your networking goals?

Creating an L&D network is also different than creating a friend group—and while the two may inevitably intersect, it's important to create networking goals aligned with your career goals and intentions. We do this by focusing on the 3 Ls: leverage, learn, and lean.

Networking Goal 1. Leverage

Your leverage goal answers the question, "What would I like my network to help me achieve?"

I want to give you permission to be a little selfish with this first networking goal. Later in this chapter, we'll discuss reciprocity and how to give back to your network, but right now, it's important to get really specific about what you'd like your network to help you achieve.

In chapter 2, we focused on setting intentions and goals, and in chapter 4, you learned how to identify your L&D niche. With those in mind, you can start pinpointing the specific opportunities your network may be able to provide. For example, if your intention is to be more mindful of a work-life balance, your network may be able to refer you to companies that align with your values. Or, maybe your recently discovered niche includes coaching—you could leverage your network to find career opportunities in which you could use that skill. For this goal, think of your network as a magical genie in a lamp—if it could grant three outcomes, what would you choose?

Networking Goal 2. Learn

Your learn goal answers the question, "What would I like to learn from my network?"

Many people think networking is all about leveraging, but you would be remiss to not see your network as an almost infinite learning resource too. Your network may provide opportunities to learn in a more social, non-formalized setting than the learning plans, certifications, and development opportunities we discussed in chapter 3. In fact, when I polled my LinkedIn audience about the "greatest gift" they'd received from their network, the overwhelming response was "knowledge."

Once you identify what you'd like to learn from your network, you can begin to seek out people, organizations, and events in your L&D niche that are aligned with your learning goals. This ensures you're not only leveraging your network against your aspirations, but also using it to grow your knowledge and expertise. For example, if your niche involves community building and cohort learning, you could follow a thought leader in that space (Nicole Papaioannou Lugara is a great example) to learn more about how they develop this type of social learning. While you may not be able to actively leverage this person to achieve a specific outcome, you can passively and actively learn from them. And that's what this goal is all about.

Networking Goal 3. Lean

Setting your lean goal answers the question, "What support do I want and need from my network?"

You will always need emotional and community support in your career journey—we all do. According to Ron Ashkenas (2016), co-author of the *Harvard Business Review Leaders Handbook*, "Managing the emotional baggage that comes with a career transition is no easy feat, no matter where you are in your career." So, while your network is great to leverage and learn from, it may also provide the emotional support you need to create a sense of ease, belonging, and community during your career transition.

Ben Duperroir (2023), a global executive business leader, calls career transitioning an "unavoidable crossroads," noting that "the uncertainty of what lies ahead can be daunting, often leading to increased stress and anxiety. It's during these transitions that our mental health can be put to the test." Ben encourages people to use their networks to navigate these crossroads because they "offer emotional support and a sense of belonging during a period that might otherwise feel isolating." Identifying how you want your network to help make you feel is key to understanding the support you want and need (or the support you anticipate needing).

> **Activity**
> Reflect on the 3 Ls (leverage, learn, and lean). Create at least one goal in each category that's aligned with your overall L&D career intentions, goals, and niche.

One big thing to keep in mind is that as your niche grows and shifts, your network will too. What you need from your network today is not what you'll need in a year, so revisit your networking goals and shift your network accordingly.

Reciprocity

While it's OK to be selfish when identifying your networking goals, particularly how you'd like to leverage your network, it's important to remember that networking is not a solo activity. "Being well connected is about reciprocity" says Alex Fish (2023). "In essence, an effective networking strategy should be seen as a two-way street."

Have you ever felt like you were the only one holding up a relationship—giving and giving but not getting anything in return? When we decide to level up our careers, it's easy to forget that feeling and default into "give me" mode. The best way to avoid temptation, and build meaningful relationships that outlast your current career position, is to use the 3 Ls to reflect on the following:

- How can your network leverage you? What do you have to offer? Can you connect?
- What can your network learn from you? What knowledge can you share with those who need it?
- How can your network lean on you? What type of emotional support can you provide for others?

> **Activity**
> Reflect on the 3 Ls and create a list of how your network can leverage, learn from, and lean on you.

It's important to remember that not everyone will need your reciprocity right now, or ever. But knowing what you have to offer ahead of time allows you to be ready to provide support to others in your network. Another way to find out how you can be of service to your network is to ask! While I know how my network can leverage, learn from, and lean on me, I always make sure to ask, "What can I do to support you?" when I'm networking with people.

The Rule of Thirds

In addition to setting goals, you want to use your goals to create a balanced network. If your network is full of people you can leverage, but very few to lean on, you'll be hard pressed to find any emotional support when you need it. Or if you have a whole network of people to learn from, but no one to help push you across the finish line of achieving your goals, you may be out of luck when you need to call in a favor or get a referral.

It's more than just balancing your network using the 3 Ls—it's about being intentional with the type of people you have inside each L. This is where the rule of thirds comes into play.

You are going to divide your network into three categories:

- **First third—your future peers.** A third of your network should align with your future peers. Once you've identified the types of roles you are looking to land next, start to connect with people who are already doing that work. This group is important because it helps you stay on top of trends, find new opportunities, and seek advice.
- **Second third—your future bosses.** A third of your network should fall into the category of the role your next boss holds. Seek out people in your network who you would report to if you landed your dream job. (Note: This isn't about finding people with open roles on their teams—it's more about connecting with your hypothetical "next boss" in terms of their title and function.) For example, if your L&D niche centers around leading L&D teams in creating leadership development programming, your future boss may be the head of L&D, a VP of L&D, or a head of people. This group is important because it provides insight into what the next level above you is thinking in terms of trends, hiring, and leadership. They are also the ones most likely to share when they have an opening on their own team.
- **Third third—your motivators.** A third of your network should be people who motivate you in any way. They may be career coaches, former colleagues, thought leaders, motivational speakers, or even people you wish to mentor or provide insights to. This group is important because it ensures you have a well-rounded network that inspires you beyond specific job titles and functions.

It's important to remember that the rule of thirds is a guideline, not a precise prescription. Ideally, you'd like each group to remain relatively balanced, but it's OK if one gets larger than another.

Meet Jen: A former marketing director, Jen was looking to make a pivot into the L&D world. She managed much of the learning function in her previous role, and she'd decided to center her new L&D niche around creating effective programs that foster employee growth, promote inclusion, and empower associates to thrive.

When we first began working together, Jen's network had a lot of marketing colleagues and junior L&D folks looking for their first job in the field. The result? She couldn't really learn from, leverage, or lean on her network for her current job search.

After revisiting her niche and thinking about the 3 Ls, Jen decided to leverage her network into referrals, learn from others about best practices for creating inclusive learning programs and lean on other marketers-turned-L&D-professionals to share their experiences and give her support. Then, she set out to build her network using the rule of thirds.

Jen began to build the first third by connecting with L&D and diversity, equity, and inclusion (DEI) program managers and directors. She focused primarily on connecting with and meeting L&D department heads, as well as people and HR team leaders to fill her second third. For her final third, Jen followed thought leaders in the marketing in L&D space, L&D career coaches, DEI practitioners and authors, and a handful of other director-level people seeking a career change into L&D.

Jen started to see the fruits of her networking labor almost immediately. She built a wonderful community of people with marketing backgrounds in L&D, received several referrals to top-tier organizations, and gained the confidence to enroll in a program to further her expertise in inclusive learning.

Your Network = Your House

Every indoor public place has to post a placard with the occupancy limit, which is the maximum amount of people allowed in that space before it becomes unsafe. Your network should have an occupancy limit too. And it's a personal decision—for some, that could be an online and real-life network of 50 people; for others, it could be more than 1,000.

In addition, just like in public places, you always have the right to refuse entry into or remove someone from your network at your own discretion. Your network is your house—you get to decide who stays and who goes.

In addition to building a new network, Jen also had to clean out her old one. She belonged to a few LinkedIn and Facebook groups for marketing professionals that no longer provided any value and were clogging up her news feeds on both platforms. Jen was also still connected with several old colleagues who didn't support her transition into L&D, and the fact that they'd see her posts always made her hesitate before publishing anything. By taking the time to block, unfollow, and remove herself from any connections or groups that no longer served her, Jen created the space to nurture a network that did.

> **Activity**
> Audit your current network using your networking goals and the rule of thirds. Remember, it's OK to remove connections, leave a networking group, or unfollow anyone who doesn't align with the network you want to build.

What's Next? Building Your Network

Now that you have gained clarity into your L&D networking goals, it's time to turn your attention to bringing them to life:

- Make sure your networking goals are written down and visible. Whenever you receive a connection request, want to send a connection request, or consider joining a networking group, ask yourself if it aligns with any of these goals.
- In the next few chapters, we'll look at how to build your L&D network ecosystem, but we can't build on something that isn't stable. Continuously audit your current network to ensure it aligns with your goals.

Chapter 10
Constructing Your L&D Network Ecosystem

SUCCESS CODES C, B & D

"Instead of better glasses, your network gives you better eyes."
—Ronald Burt

As our world has become exponentially more digital, our ability to network has changed too. We can use our phones to connect with peers, colleagues, and thought leaders from around the world. Networking is no longer limited to sanctioned, local events—we now have endless opportunities to build a holistic, digital-first network.

However, these endless opportunities can also be overwhelming. Whether you have a natural aversion to networking, don't think you have the time to dedicate to it, or don't know where to start, I encourage you to think of networking as a marathon, not a sprint. As my mom (and Grand Pabbie) says, it's about doing "the next right thing" versus trying to solve everything at once. By taking incremental steps to build a network that's aligned with your networking goals, you'll craft an intentional network without even realizing it.

Building Your L&D Network Ecosystem

Your network is a living, breathing manifestation of how you interact with the world to gain connections, insights, and develop professional and social skills. Like any ecosystem, your L&D network doesn't survive in a vacuum; it requires nurturing from seven different sources: current connections, connections of connections, LinkedIn, free online groups, paid communities, events and meetups, and professional associations (Figure 10-1).

Figure 10-1. Your L&D Network Ecosystem

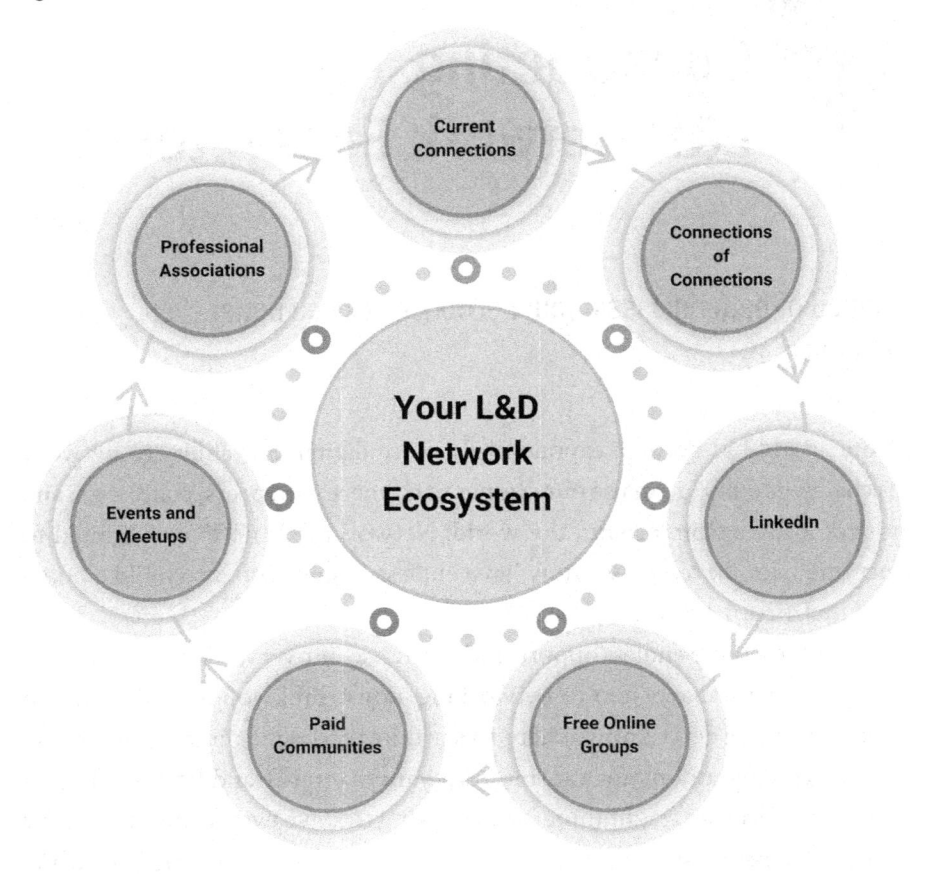

Your L&D Network Ecosystem, with nodes: Current Connections, Connections of Connections, LinkedIn, Free Online Groups, Paid Communities, Events and Meetups, Professional Associations.

When you look at these areas, however, it's important to remember that you don't need to focus on all seven to build a successful network. If you already have a decent number of people in your network, for example, you might want to start by reviewing your current connections. If you want to grow your network in a group setting, start by joining a community or professional association. If you're short on time, see what LinkedIn or Facebook groups you can join and focus on spending a few minutes each day inside those groups. No matter where you start, keeping your networking goals at the forefront of your mind will help ensure you're constructing an aligned and intentional network.

Now, let's explore each area in more detail.

Current Connections

When you look back at your networking goals from chapter 9, which of your current connections could you leverage, learn from, or lean on? Or do you think you'll need to build a whole new network around these goals?

When creating a strong network, most people forget to start with the network they already have. While not everyone in your network will align with your new goals, you'd be remiss to ignore anyone who's already an active part of your network. This could include LinkedIn connections, former and current peers and colleagues you are still in touch with, former supervisors you still have a relationship with, fellow university alumni, and so on.

So, before you start adding people to your network, review your current connections and identify anyone who still aligns with your networking goals.

> **Meet Erin:** Erin, a former customer success manager, was looking to get into the consulting side of L&D. As she built her network, she went through her current connections to see if anyone worked for a consulting firm—either for a referral (leverage) or to learn more about making the transition into the consulting world (learn). As she was scrolling on LinkedIn, she saw that a colleague from her K–12 education days was now an L&D consultant at a large consulting firm—in the city she was looking to relocate to! She sent him a message, they hopped on a call to catch up, and he referred her to a role. A few weeks later, after a handful of interviews, Erin was offered a job as a senior L&D consultant.

Connections of Connections

A few years ago, I was on a networking call with a man named Moshe who wanted to learn more about the work I was doing as an L&D director in the real estate industry. At the end of our call, rather than hanging up, Moshe thanked me for my time and asked me to share two or three additional people he should connect with. I immediately thought of two of my former colleagues and offered to connect them to make it more personal. Those colleagues then referred two to three additional people for him to talk to, and soon enough, he had built a large network and following—all because he asked that question at the end of each networking conversation.

The quickest way to grow your network is to parlay the current connections you have into new connections. You can do this by asking your current connections to recommend a handful of people for you to connect with based on your networking goals. Another option is to use a platform such as LinkedIn to see if you have anyone in common with potential connections and then ask that common denominator to provide an introduction.

> **Meet Joanna:** A senior instructional designer looking for her next managerial ID role, Joanna was searching for other high-level IDs to connect with on LinkedIn when she stumbled across a post from one. After reading the post, she knew she wanted to connect with this person, so she took a few minutes to look for any mutual connections. I was a mutual connection and was able to introduce them in a group message on LinkedIn. From there, they had a great conversation that turned into an eventual referral for Joanna!

LinkedIn (New Connections)

At the time of this publication, LinkedIn has about 1 billion users from all around the world, which makes it an incredible resource for forming relationships and meeting people you may never cross paths with otherwise.

Reaching out to new connections can be a little intimidating, however, especially if you don't have a mutual connection. In addition, while a database of a billion people is quite the resource, it can feel like looking for a needle in a haystack when you're trying to find people to connect with.

One aligned, intentional way to find new connections is to use LinkedIn's "search people" function and leverage your niche statement and networking goals. To do this, grab two to three keywords from your niche statement or goals, create a Boolean search with those keywords (using AND in between each), and then filter by "people." This will bring up anyone who has those words in their headlines. Alternatively, filtering by "posts" would highlight any posts that contain those keywords. For example, if your niche statement refers to your skills and interests in coaching, program management, and data analysis, and one of your networking goals is to learn more about effective learning measurement techniques, you could use coaching, data analysis, and measurement as your search terms.

Meet Spencer: Spencer was a former K–12 educator turned sales trainer looking to couple a PhD in learning technologies with his passion for program development. His niche statement was "I develop and ideate modern technology-led learning strategies and programs by leveraging strategic thinking, curriculum development, and analysis for collaborative and forward-thinking organizations."

With most of his LinkedIn connections in the education world, Spencer knew he'd need to create new connections to grow his L&D career. From his niche statement and goals, Spencer pulled out "learning technology," "analysis," and "curriculum development," and searched for both "people" and "posts" on LinkedIn. Within an hour, he had sent out 10 connection requests, and one had already accepted his request for a Zoom coffee chat.

Free Online Groups

It's true that "your network is your net worth," but you don't have to spend your whole net worth to build a network. In fact, there are tens of thousands of free online groups in the L&D field that you can join and create meaningful connections in. At the time of this publication, LinkedIn has more than 11,000 free groups in the L&D category, and Facebook has thousands more. While a free online group isn't the same as a community (that's coming up next), these online groups can provide a great gateway to creating one-on-one connections by serving as a soft-opener to reach out to other group members.

Meet Stacey: As a former educator looking to transition into L&D for the first time, Stacey joined a free LinkedIn group for L&D professionals. Not knowing where to start on her L&D career journey, Stacey posted about looking for support. I was also a member of that group, and I reached out as soon as I saw Stacey's post. I had just launched my coaching practice and was looking for my first client—and Stacey agreed to be that person!

Less than 90 days after we started working together, Stacey landed a senior instructional designer and trainer role at a healthcare organization (where she has since been promoted twice). Our paths may have never crossed if Stacey hadn't joined and posted in that LinkedIn group.

Structured Communities (Paid and Unpaid)

While online groups are less structured and typically focused on peer-to-peer support and interactions with light moderation, communities are more structured, created around a specific focus, and provide programming, resources, community events, and so forth.

Structured communities also typically have a fee structure, although some are offered for free. They're great to join if you are a little more averse to "blindly" reaching out to new people on LinkedIn (or in real life) and would rather be part of a group than have a one-to-one interaction. While these communities serve as great breeding grounds for professional relationships, they also provide additional learning opportunities and targeted support, which means they'll likely be able to help you achieve your 3 Ls.

Here are a few of my favorite communities and their geographic regions:
- The Global Learning and Development Community (global)
- The Training, Learning, and Development Community (US)*
- L&D Shakers (Europe)
- The L&D Forum (Australia)
- The L&D Collective by 360Learning (Global)
- L&D Cares (US)
- LRN DEV REV (Global)*
- Offbeat (Global)*

These are either paid communities or have options to pay for specific community upgrades.

> **Meet Valeriia:** As a seasoned HR professional, Valeriia had years of experience in training and development. When she came to me, she'd decided to fully focus her career in the L&D space. Most of her network held HR generalist roles and couldn't help her get to the next level in her career. Because she was living in Amsterdam and craved a sense of community to learn from in Europe, Valeriia joined the L&D Shakers community. She immediately started attending live and virtual events to learn from her peers across Europe. Joining the L&D Shakers community gave Valeriia the confidence to apply for roles in the L&D field, and she ultimately landed her dream L&D role. Immediately after landing that role, Valeriia decided to give back to the community that had given her so much—now she facilitates live programs, events, and community discussions.

Events and Conferences (Online or In-Person)

Events and conferences offer real-time connection, provide the opportunity to learn about the latest trends, and give you access to industry thought leaders and experts. Attending events and conferences is one of the only ways to build your network while simultaneously hitting all three networking goals at once.

Many of the communities I shared earlier, as well as the memberships and associations listed in the next section, offer conferences that even nonmembers can attend. According to Mobilo (2023), here's what you should consider before selecting an event or conference:
- Research the event, looking into past speakers, attendee feedback, and online reviews.
- Consider whether the cost fits your budget and matches the value you'll get out of attending.
- Evaluate the schedule to ensure you can actually attend.
- Make sure networking opportunities are built into the event (for example, ATD's International Conference & EXPO has a Networking Night event that's dedicated solely to networking).
- Understand how the event or conference aligns with your networking goals.

Meet Rebecca: Rebecca, a former university senior lecturer, was looking to make her first official entrance into the corporate L&D world, but most of her network was previous higher-education peers. After joining some structured online communities, Rebecca realized she wanted to meet L&D professionals in a live setting. So, she started attending local L&D Shakers events in New York City; she enjoyed them so much she even volunteered to host them. After joining and hosting several local events, Rebecca received not one, but two job offers solely through her networking.

Memberships and Associations

Membership and associations take communities to the next level. Typically, associations offer an elevated level of programming and individualized networking opportunities for members. Most L&D memberships and communities are run by dedicated teams who focus on the community aspect and provide additional levels of support and content.

Associations like ATD offer both national and regional support, allowing you to make connections and benefit from their resources nationally, while also connecting locally with other L&D professionals. It's the best of both worlds.

> **Meet Amanda:** Amanda was a former e-learning developer looking for her next opportunity in the L&D space, preferably focused on e-learning design and LMS administration. She'd leveraged her network in the past to land roles, so she once again turned to her network. This time, rather than focusing on one-to-one connections, Amanda created deeper community connections and programming. She joined and quickly started volunteering with a local ATD chapter. This allowed her to connect with several people who had open LMS administrator positions in their organizations; she also received quite a few referrals. Even after landing her dream L&D role, Amanda stayed on as a volunteer VP, overseeing chapter programming to pay it forward.

Activity
Identify two to three areas you'd like to focus on as you start to build your L&D network ecosystem. Create a plan to put those into practice today.

Now that you've built this potent network, you need an inner circle you can tap into at any time for support and guidance. How do you do this? You build a personal board of directors.

Building Your Personal Board of Directors

It's one thing to have a deep network; it's another to be able to call on someone the moment you need them. Your personal board of directors (PBOD) is designed to help you achieve goals, provide you with timely feedback, hold you accountable when needed, and help you navigate challenging situations that come up in your L&D career. Just as an organization looks to its board for guidance and direction, you'll go to these people whenever you need their support (Figure 10-2).

Figure 10-2. Your Personal Board of Directors

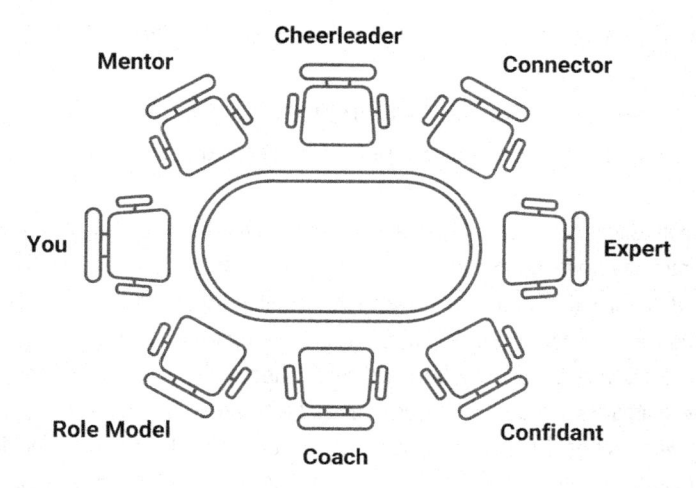

[Diagram: An oval table surrounded by eight chairs labeled: You, Mentor, Cheerleader, Connector, Expert, Confidant, Coach, Role Model]

Your PBOD is made up of you (because you need to sit on your own board) and seven other people:

- **The mentor** is a person with experience in your field who can guide you through your career path by offering advice and helping you navigate professional challenges.
- **The cheerleader** is an enthusiastic supporter who believes in your potential and encourages you during the high and low points of your career journey.
- **The connector** is a well-networked individual who can open doors for you by making introductions to influencers and potential employers in the industry.
- **The expert** is a knowledgeable specialist in an L&D area who can share current insights, trends, and deep expertise to inform your decisions and strategies.
- **The confidant** is a trustworthy individual you can speak with candidly about your career aspirations, fears, and secrets without fear of judgment or breach of confidentiality.
- **The coach** is a professional who is focused on helping you develop your skills, define your career goals, and create a plan to achieve them through structured advice and accountability.

- **The role model** is someone who embodies the success and attributes you aspire to develop and serves as a guiding example in your professional life.

Each of these positions hold different responsibilities, so you want to fill all seven seats. However, the same person may hold one or more seats.

> **Meet Glenn:** Glenn was a former L&D manager and change management practitioner looking for a career challenge in the leadership development field. He had reached the final round for two great roles (both overseeing leadership development), and knew he'd likely have to decide between the two. Rather than spiraling down a decision-making hole, Glenn asked his board for advice. Specifically, he called on his cheerleader, expert, role model, and coach (me). He shared his thoughts with each of us and listened to our advice and feedback. After meeting with his board, Glenn was able to confidently choose the right role for him. (Coincidentally, Glenn was the one who introduced me to the concept of having a PBOD.)

Unlike an organization's board of directors, your PBOD does not have to meet quarterly. In fact, you don't even have to tell people that they're on your PBOD. They're simply meant to be a group of people you know you can leverage, lean on, and learn from when you need them.

> **Activity**
> Identify and reach out to individuals who can fill the seven seats on your personal board of directors: mentor, cheerleader, connector, expert, confidant, coach, and role model. They will provide support, guidance, and accountability as you navigate your L&D career. Regularly engage with them for advice and feedback to help achieve your professional goals.

What's Next? Leveraging and Maintaining Your L&D Network Ecosystem

Your network ecosystem, just like any living organism, needs nurturing to grow. Maintain your network ecosystem by taking these steps:
- Make sure to give your network as much as you take. Remember, you are building long-term relationships, not short-term gains, so you

should focus how you can be of service to them in addition to what they can do for you.
- Don't stop networking once you reach your L&D career goal. This is one of the biggest mistakes people make. Continue to prioritize networking and shift your ecosystem to fit your niche. If you do, the next time you're in the market for a new role, your nurtured ecosystem will be ready to fast track your process.

To start putting this chapter's concepts into action, consider how you can:
- Leverage your existing connections by reaching out to colleagues and alumni who align with your goals for catch-up calls and potential referrals.
- Expand your network by asking current contacts to introduce you to additional people and using LinkedIn to find mutual connections.
- Join and actively participate in two to three online L&D groups or communities to build new connections and gain industry insights.

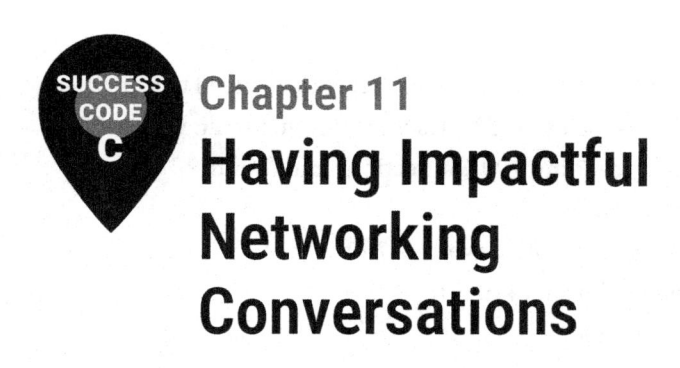

Chapter 11
Having Impactful Networking Conversations

SUCCESS CODE C

"Conversation is a meeting of minds with different memories and habits. When minds meet, they don't just exchange facts; they transform them, reshape them, draw different implications from them, engage in new trains of thought. Conversation doesn't just reshuffle the cards: It creates new cards." —Theodore Zeldin

If you've just finished reading the two previous chapters, you may be thinking, "OK, I've built this awesome network that I can leverage, learn from, and lean on—but how can I make sure our conversations are fruitful once I actually connect with them?" That's a great question. It's one thing to build a network that aligns with your L&D career goals and aspirations, but it's another to actually engage them.

You'll need to prepare three things before you start engaging with your network: sample connection prompts, your elevator pitch, and goal-aligned questions you would like answered.

Sample Connection Prompts

In chapter 10, you learned how to find people to include in your goal-aligned L&D network ecosystem. But how do you get them to go from being strangers to being part of your ecosystem? What do you say to them in your initial outreach?

If you're connecting with someone new online, you will need to send them a connection request. Chris Skees (2023), learning product manager at Cisco Meraki, ran an A/B test by sending 100 connections and found:
- 50 requests with no note:
  - 94 percent accepted within a week (47 of 50)
  - 8 percent messaged back (4 of 50)
- 50 requests with a personalized note:
  - 64 percent accepted within a week (32 of 50)
  - 46 percent messaged back (23 of 50)
  - 71 percent of those who accepted messaged back (23 of 32 accepted invitations)

What this data shows, says Skees, is that "if you want to grow your network, send connection requests without a note. If you want to start conversations, send connection requests with a hyper-personalized note."

As we've already discussed several times in this book, quality, not quantity, is what's important when building a network you can leverage, learn from, and lean on. Personalized notes help you create these quality connections.

What makes a note personalized? If you're sending it as part of a connection request (LinkedIn, for example, allows you to add a note *alongside* your request), you only have 200 characters to work with. A personalized note shows you took the time to review their profile, read some of their posts (if they actively post), and connect the dots as to why they belong in your L&D network ecosystem. Here are some examples:
- "Chris, I really loved your perspective on Ross Stevenson's post about applying AI for L&D in your org. Would love to connect with you to learn more about your process!"
- "Hi Amanda! Your career journey is really inspiring! I'd love to connect to learn more about how you made the jump from science teacher (I was one too!) to head of CS in less than five years."
- "Hi Brandon, I'm researching my next career move and L&D project manager keeps coming up. I see you've been in that role for two years, and I would love to connect with likeminded people in the space!"

> **Activity**
> Run your own test! Find five to 10 people you'd like to have a conversation with and send them a personalized note. Look for any trends, what seemed to work, and what didn't. Use the notes that worked as a template for future connections.

Your Networking Elevator Pitch

What is your immediate response when someone new says, "Tell me a little bit about yourself"? If you want to shrink and hide, you're not alone. According to two research studies on social fears and phobias, 26.5 percent of people fear or have a phobia of meeting new people, while 21.2 percent have a fear or phobia of talking to strangers (Ruscio et al. 2023).

Fortunately, meeting and talking to new people is a skill that can be honed with practice. Your first task is to learn how to properly introduce yourself—and that's where the elevator pitch comes in. According to the University of California, Davis Internship and Career Center, the goal of your elevator pitch "is to introduce yourself, engage your audience and to start a conversation. [It] needs to quickly convey important information." The more confident you are as you start the conversation, the more confident you'll be during the conversation.

The best elevator pitches focus on four main parts, which build on one another: your intro, origin story, career overview, and what's next (Figure 11-1).

Figure 11-1. Your Four-Part Networking Elevator Pitch

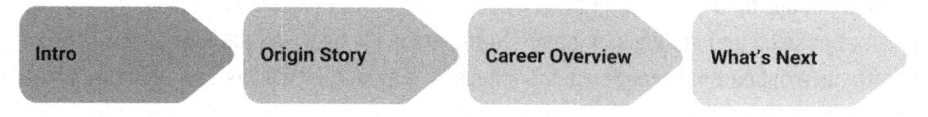

Intro → Origin Story → Career Overview → What's Next

Part 1. Intro

The best introductions pull someone in. Rather than diving headfirst into your career history, you want to begin introducing yourself by using your niche statement to provide a brief overview of your niche. This gives you and the person you're talking to a chance to immediately connect on a deeper level, while also quickly getting to the heart of who you are and what you're about.

> **Meet Emma:** When transitioning into L&D from higher education, Emma knew she wanted to focus on developing and managing onboarding programs. As an academic and career advisor in charge of helping students find work, she knew firsthand how effective the onboarding experience was, especially for those early in their careers. Having experienced some great (and not so great) onboarding experiences herself, Emma landed on this L&D niche statement:
>
>> I design and lead early career onboarding programs by leveraging facilitation, relationship building, and content development for organizations that value diversity.
>
> So, when Emma developed her intro, she used her niche statement to kick off each conversation like this:
>
>> I'm enthusiastic about designing and leading early career onboarding programs and being able to use my facilitation, relationship building, and content development skills inside organizations that value diversity.

Part 2. Origin Story

Now that you've pulled them in, you want to keep them there by briefly mentioning where your enthusiasm comes from. This pulls from your why (from chapter 4) and allows you to quickly connect on a deeper level with the person you're talking to.

> To relay her personal experiences and the firsthand accounts she'd heard from students about their onboarding experiences, Emma told those she was connecting with "that passion and enthusiasm stems from personally being on the receiving end of an effective onboarding experience that shaped my career, as well as seeing firsthand the influence onboarding has in creating preparedness, connection, and comfort for those early in their career."

Your origin story gives the person you are speaking to something compelling to connect with you over. According to the US National Institutes of Health, "compelling narratives cause oxytocin release and have the power to affect our attitudes, beliefs, and behaviors" (Zak 2015). Furthermore, the research goes on to say that oxytocin "is synthesized in the human brain when one is trusted," causing the person on the receiving end of your conversation to actually feel closer to you, even if you aren't in the same room or have never met before.

Part 3. Career Overview

Now that the oxytocin is flowing, it's time to hit them with a handful of career accomplishments (in chronological order). This serves to back up your intro and origin story with tangible facts and data. According to a Medical News Today article, "To the brain, information is its own reward," meaning that providing information to further support the first two parts of your pitch will set off reward sensors in the brain (Cohut 2019). This creates the feeling of it being a "rewarding" conversation.

You can kick off your career overview using this formula:

> "My career began with my role as [*insert role*] where I used [*insert two to three skills*] to [*insert one to two specific achievements or examples*]."

You'll want to continue recapping your career path using your own version of this formula (feel free to take your own creative liberty with it), until you reach your most recent role.

> Now that Emma had created a sense of connection with those she was networking with, they were excited to hear a little more about her career history:
>
> My career began with my role as an educator, where I used my curriculum design and development skills to create more than 50 unique lesson plans and modules per year, which increased overall student engagement by more than 20 percent. Looking for a bigger challenge, I took on a new role as an assistant academic and career advisor. There, I coached students to choose their internships—it was the first time many of them had worked in a professional setting, so I focused on increasing their overall job satisfaction year over year. From there, I was promoted into my current role as an academic advisor where I can better use my coaching and facilitation skills. I've successfully led virtual one-on-one and group onboarding sessions for more than 1,000 early career students and new grads.

Part 4. What's Next

It's time for the grand conclusion of your pitch—your hopes for the future and your goals. A lot of elevator pitches go wrong because they end with the career overview and something like, "So, yeah, that's me." The problem with this abrupt ending is that it hands the conversation back to the other person before you can clearly articulate what you hope to accomplish by speaking to them.

I suggest taking a look at your networking goals and deciding which ones you're hoping to achieve by starting this relationship. For example, are you hoping to leverage this person into a referral? Do you want to learn more about a specific type of role? Are you looking for like-minded people to lean on? Knowing this ahead of time will allow you to customize your what's next section for each person you're networking with.

Here are three sample formulas you can use for your what's next, depending on your networking goals:

- **When you're looking to leverage:** "And now I'm looking for a [*type of role*] for a company that values [*two to three values*], where I can really use my [*two to three skills*] to [*first part of your niche*]. This has led me to our conversation today."
- **When you're looking to learn:** "And now I'm looking to connect with people who [*why you connected with them*] to learn more about [*what you want to learn more about*]. This has led me to our conversation today.
- **When you're looking to lean on:** "And now I'm looking for like-minded people who [*why you connected with them*] to connect with and create a mutual support network. This has led me to our conversation today."

> When Emma first began her networking journey, her priority was to focus on her learn networking goals. She wanted to understand how she could leverage and use her facilitation, project management, and analysis skills as she made her transition from higher education to the corporate L&D space. As she looked for people who were primarily focused on onboarding, the what's next part of her elevator pitch ended with:

> And now I'm looking to connect with people in L&D program manager roles to learn more about how to best use my facilitation, project management, and analysis skills to build next-level onboarding programs. This has led me to our conversation today.

Once Emma started to achieve this networking goal, she began pivoting her conversations to her leverage goal. She started networking with people who had shared open roles on their teams or were connected inside and to organizations she admired and wanted to work for. Her what's next then shifted to:

> And now I'm looking for an L&D program manager role for a company that values feedback, creativity, and diversity, where I can really use my facilitation, project management, and analysis skills to build next-level onboarding programs. This has led me to our conversation today.

By tailoring her what's next section to her networking goal and the person she was talking to, Emma was able to give them a clear picture of what she wanted to achieve. It was through a connection of a connection that Emma kicked off a conversation with her now manager and landed her dream L&D role overseeing organization-wide onboarding.

Elevator Pitch Best Practices

Here are a few tips and tricks for creating the best elevator pitch:

- **Timing.** Shoot for your elevator pitch to be less than five minutes (two to four minutes is the sweet spot). Because most networking conversations last about 30 minutes, this leaves 80 to 85 percent of the call time for asking questions and conversing in a more two-way manner.
- **Combining experiences.** If you've held the same role at a few organizations, you can combine them into one career experience in your career overview. For example, I was head of L&D for a few years at a few different organizations, but my job functions were essentially the same. So, rather than listing each one, I combined them by saying, "From there I went on to be a head of learning for several different retail, consulting, and real-estate organizations over the next seven years."

- **Length**. For a work history with more than five unique roles, either combine experiences or focus on one main accomplishment per role (otherwise, your timing could be way off). If your work history has four or fewer unique roles, feel free to expand on additional accomplishments or share how your role and responsibilities shifted while in each role.
- **Practice**. Once you write your elevator pitch, practice it often! The best tip is to record yourself saying it and then listen to the recording until you've memorized it in a more conversational way. Practice your speech with your personal board of directors or someone you trust to give you feedback.

> **Activity**
> Craft a concise and compelling elevator pitch that includes an engaging introduction, a brief origin story, a career overview, and a clear statement of what you're looking to achieve next. Practice delivering your pitch until you can present it confidently and naturally in less than five minutes. Pro tip: Use your insights from chapters 3 and 4 to focus on the skills, interests, and values you bring to the table.

Asking Goal-Aligned Questions

The biggest mistake I see people make when networking with someone for the first time is immediately asking this virtual stranger to do something for them. I often liken networking to dating—if you're single and going about your day and someone comes up to you and abruptly asks for your phone number, would you give it to them? I doubt it. However, if this person approaches you in a respectful manner, strikes up a good two-way conversation, is intrigued to learn more about you and who you are, and you decide you also have a genuine interest in them, it's much more likely that you'll give them your phone number at the end of that conversation.

Same goes for networking—although not romantic, networking does foster relationships that require courting and nurturing. The networking equivalent of asking a stranger for their number while they're crossing the street is to immediately ask them to refer you to their organization, review your resume, or perform any additional task for you. Those tasks must be offered or earned, not requested immediately—unless you're looking to turn off the person you're trying to connect with.

So, how do you reach your networking goals without turning off the people you're networking with? First, remember that networking is a marathon, not a sprint. Relationships typically don't happen overnight and it takes time to develop a connection that bears fruits for both parties.

In addition, you should ask goal-aligned questions that are focused on them. Let's look at some examples:

- **If your *leverage networking goal* is to get a referral for a specific organization**, don't ask, "Can you please refer me to your organization?" Instead, say something like, "The company you work for is really intriguing to me because it looks like it highly values creativity and forward-thinking. What drew you to want to work there and what keeps you there? What do you think makes for a good culture fit or add to the company?"
- **If your *learn networking goal* is to learn how to make the career transition from individual contributor to manager**, don't say, "What should I do to make the leap from individual contributor to manager?" Instead, say, "I see you moved from individual contributor to manager less than a year into your last role. What prepared you to make that move, and what weren't you prepared for that you wish you had been?"
- **If your *learn networking goal* is to find a like-minded community to discuss specific job-related challenges**, avoid saying, "Where can I go to meet more people who have these challenges?" Instead, ask, "What are the biggest challenges you face in your role, and where do you seek outside support to overcome them?"

A few additional questions you can ask include:
- What was your path to get to the role you're in now?
- What does a typical day look like for you?

- What are the biggest challenges you face in your role, and what skills do you rely on to overcome them?
- What was your journey in mastering [*insert skill or skills*]?
- How do you use [*insert skill or skills*] on a day-to-day basis?
- What support did you receive during your career that made a big difference for you?

As you can see, these questions show that you have a genuine interest in the person you're connecting with while also being completely honest about your networking intentions. Typically, once you've established a genuine level of rapport and trust, you can then proceed with a specific ask you may need or desire.

> **Activity**
> Create your own sample list of goal-aligned questions to ask during your next networking interaction.

What's Next? Connecting With Your Network

The beautiful thing about networking is that it will always work out in your favor: you just never know when. To make sure you get the most out of your networking connections, start with the following:

- Write your elevator pitch, incorporating your niche statement, origin story, career overview, and what's next. Practice delivering it until you feel comfortable.
- Create a list of goal-aligned questions to ask during networking conversations, focusing on learning from others' experiences and building genuine connections.

PART 4
Mastering the L&D Job Search Process

Chapter 12
Interview Preparedness

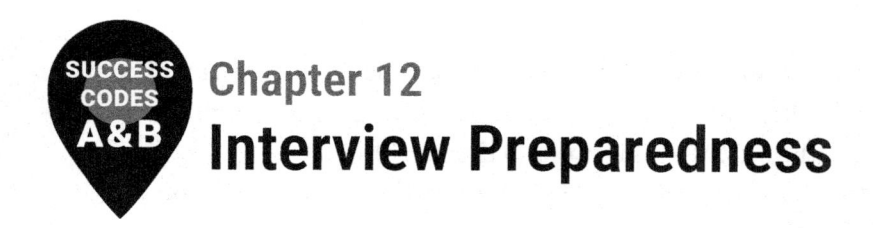

"I believe luck is preparation meeting opportunity. If you hadn't been prepared when the opportunity came along, you wouldn't have been lucky." —Oprah Winfrey

When it comes to any job transition—whether it's one you've been actively pursuing or just dabbling in passively—interviewing is one of the most stressful parts of the process. If you're starting to sweat even thinking about interviewing, you're not alone. In a 2020 study of more than 2,000 job seekers, a whopping 93 percent said they experienced interview-related anxiety (JDP 2020).

The good news is that preparation is the absolute best antidote for interview anxiety, and it's important to understand that you can (and should) start to prepare before you even have an interview on the books. In the next three chapters, we'll explore how to show up as your best, most confident and knowledgeable self by approaching interviews in three parts:

- **Overall preparation** involves preparing yourself mentally for heading into the interview stage of the career evolution process and is the focus of this chapter. This part includes avoiding overpreparing, identifying your interview red and green flags, preparing your elevator pitch, and crafting your interview stories.
- **Specific interview prep** involves putting your interview stories to use by aligning them to the job description and specifications. This is 10 times easier once you've done your overall preparation. We'll cover this in chapter 13.

- **Post-interview** you've still got work to do. Preparing a thank-you note template, along with any aligning work samples, will help you seal the deal. We'll cover this in chapter 14.

Before we dive in, here's a question for you: Is your instinct to rehearse every possible question when preparing for an interview? If so, you're not alone. It's logical to believe that by curating the "perfect" response, you will become more desirable to the interviewer. However, the meticulous rehearsal of often arbitrary interview questions may be the kiss of death for your interview—it often hinders your chances more than helping them.

Over-preparation is the number 1 thing that can strip the baseline of trust from your interactions. According to Frances Frei (2020), professor at Harvard Business School, trust relies on three areas working together:

- **Logic.** I know you can do it; your reasoning and judgement are sound.
- **Empathy.** I believe you care about me and my success.
- **Authenticity.** I experience the real you.

The Trust Triangle model is technically focused on developing trust across organizations, but when I heard Frei deliver a keynote about it in summer 2023, I couldn't help but see a direct correlation to building trust during an interview. At the end of the day, the people interviewing you want to experience the real you (authenticity), know you can do the job (logic), and believe you care about the success of their organization (empathy).

When you over prepare, it's easy to become overly rehearsed and come across robotic and inauthentic, obscuring your true personality. Focusing too much on saying the right thing often keeps you from engaging in deeper dialogue, which in turn may keep the interaction surface level. Just remember, hiring managers and peers want to have a genuine exchange of ideas and information so they can determine if you're the right fit for their team.

While coaching hundreds of clients through the interview process, I've found that those who over prepare tend to struggle to pivot or engage deeply with unexpected questions. This rigidity in preparation ends up being a disadvantage, especially if it causes you to feel flustered in the moment. When you're just prepared enough (rather than overprepared), you can showcase your true logic, authenticity, and empathy.

With all that said, it's still very easy to slip into over-preparation mode, especially for a role that really excites you. Here are a handful of warning signs that you're heading into that territory:

- **Feeling like you're memorizing a script.** If you find yourself spending hours memorizing answers to potential interview questions, to the point where you're basically rehearsing lines for a play, you might be over preparing.
- **Anxiety when deviating from prepared answers.** If the thought of being asked a question that requires you to pivot from your prepared answers causes significant anxiety, this is a sign of overpreparation.
- **Lack of engagement in practice or mock interviews.** If you're unable to engage in a natural conversation during a practice interview because you're trying to remember specific answers, that's a sign you're too focused on giving prepackaged answers instead of engaging in a dialogue that builds trust.

Over preparing can lead to physical and mental burnout, which can also influence your interview performance. If any of this resonates with you, you've likely already entered overpreparation mode. However, it's not too late to pump the brakes! Take a deep breath, walk away from the canned responses, and recommit to bringing your most authentic self to interviews.

Identifying Your Interview Red and Green Flags

If you take nothing else from this chapter, I want you to remember this: Even if it doesn't feel like it, wherever you are in the interview process, you are interviewing them just as much (if not more) than they are interviewing you.

Even in the most competitive job markets, it's important to hold your ground on what you need and want in the next stage of your career. To do this, start by determining your interview red and green flags.

We all know what a red flag is—a warning of danger. An interview red flag would include any concerning sign or indicator that the company, role, hiring manager, or work environment is not a good fit or that it doesn't align with your values, needs, and expectations. It's important to flush out this list prior to beginning the interview process so you can be hyper aware of what to look out for.

To identify your red flags, ask yourself these questions:
- How will you know there is *not* a value alignment with this role or company?
- What will it feel like when you meet a leader you *don't* want to work for?
- How *don't* you want to feel after each interview?
- What behaviors will you see that let you know this is *not* the right role for you?

On the flip side, it's equally as important to identify your green flags—signs that the company, role, hiring manager, and work environment are a good fit for you. While many people skip this step, identifying your green flags allows you to make sure you're not settling just because you didn't see any red flags.

To identify your green flags, ask yourself these questions:
- How will you know there is a value alignment with a role or company?
- What will it feel like when you meet a leader you want to work for?
- How do you want to feel after each interview?
- What behaviors will you see that let you know this is the right role, company, or team for you?

Once you've developed this list, keep it close and revisit it after each interview. Your green flags should serve as your guideposts during the interview process to ensure you're directing your energy toward roles, organizations, and teams that align with your skills, interests, strengths, and values.

Developing Your Interview Elevator Pitch

Now that you know how to avoid the pitfalls of over preparing and how to look out for both warning and encouraging signs that you and the organization you're interviewing with are aligned, it's time to prepare your interview elevator pitch.

Your elevator pitch is essentially the answer to "tell me a little about yourself" or "walk me through your experience." It's similar to the networking elevator pitch you developed in chapter 11, but this one shifts focus slightly to include why you're right for the role. Because it is often the first thing an interviewer hears from you, my philosophy is that your elevator pitch should answer more questions than it asks by highlighting your key strengths, accomplishments, and the unique value you can bring to the organization.

A successful interview elevator pitch hits four main areas:

- **Timing**. Ideally you want to keep your elevator pitch to about five minutes. A typical virtual interview is 30 to 45 minutes (depending on the round), and you can expect a typical in-person interview to last anywhere from 45 minutes to more than an hour (Hinnkle 2023). With that said, you can include some wiggle room in your five-minute elevator pitch so you can expand on parts if your interview is longer.
- **Confidence**. One of the biggest confidence hacks when delivering your elevator pitch is to use "me" more than "we." While you want to highlight examples of how you contributed to a team, it's also important to take credit for and showcase results you achieved individually. Another way to show confidence is to avoid using too many qualifiers (such as *even though, kind of, just,* or *only*), which dilute the strength of your statement. Focus on removing qualifiers from your vocabulary, especially in your elevator pitch.
- **Alignment**. Your elevator pitch isn't a laundry list of everything you've ever done—it's a carefully curated story of how your experience aligns with your niche, showcasing not only what you've achieved, but what you want to continue achieving. It should give the interviewer a glimpse into your career highlights and your next career move.
- **Storytelling**. Last, your elevator pitch should share a cohesive story that follows a logical progression and gives just enough

context without overwhelming the recipient. As we'll explore later in this chapter when we discuss developing your interview stories, storytelling creates a strong connection and has the power to engage the interviewer emotionally, making your pitch more memorable.

Elevator Pitch Structure

When we discussed your networking elevator pitch in chapter 11, you structured it around four elements: intro, origin story, career overview, and what's next. You'll use that same structure for your interview elevator pitch, but you'll make some tweaks to the third and fourth parts (Figure 12-1).

Figure 12-1. The 4 Parts to Your Interview Elevator Pitch

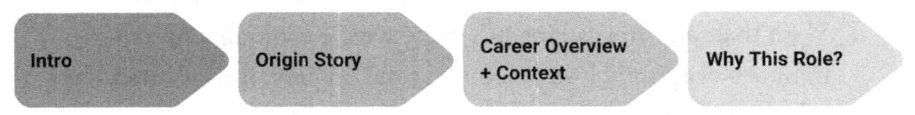

Intro → Origin Story → Career Overview + Context → Why This Role?

Note: If you haven't had a chance to explore chapter 11, I highly recommend doing that now before moving forward in this chapter.

Career Overview

While you can start with your intro and origin story from your networking elevator pitch, you'll layer on to them by adding more color to each role. In addition to sharing your highlights and accomplishments, you should also add:

- **Challenges.** No role is all rainbows and sunshine—your future employer wants to know you can handle pivots and challenges because they are bound to occur. Make sure to include some of the challenges you faced in each role you share.
- **Context.** While you still want to highlight your skills, it's important to add context to your pitch. Beyond sharing what skills you used, add in how you used them. Keep it high level, as you will dive into the nuances in your interview stories.

Meet Sarah: With more than a decade of L&D experience, Sarah was looking for a new L&D role focused specifically within her niche (leadership development) for rapidly scaling organizations. When she was networking, she would share this career overview about one of her roles:

> I was brought over as the first director of corporate training. I focused on using my learning strategy, program management, and executive coaching skills to develop high-level leadership development programs, doubling overall trust in executives in just 90 days.

As she was preparing for her interviews, she wanted to showcase her ability to successfully design and lead high-level programming, so she tweaked the career overview by adding challenges and context:

> I then came over as one of the first L&D hires, reporting directly into the head of leadership and learning, and became the first ever director of corporate training. We had just experienced a huge growth spurt both geographically and in headcount, and many people became leaders out of necessity rather than readiness, which caused a lot of confusion, tension, and lack of trust. I focused my time there on competency-based leadership development programming—specifically for developing high-level leaders. I used my learning strategy, program management, and executive coaching skills to create programming designed to first onboard them into their leadership roles, and then grow their executive skills and capabilities. Just 90 days after implementing the first round of programming, employee trust in leadership doubled. The program was so successful in ramping up leadership development among new executives that it's still running today!

As you can see, including the challenges and additional context adds a deeper storytelling aspect to your elevator pitch, and allows the recipient to see how your experience aligns with what they need someone to do in the role. Using this model will help create an emotional connection between you and the interviewer, because they can find key points in your elevator pitch that resonate with them.

Hot tip: Similar to your networking elevator pitch, you can combine experiences if you have a longer work history. For example, because I worked for two consulting firms back-to-back, I combined them into one in my interview elevator pitch by starting with, "I then held a global learning consultant role at two consulting firms where I . . ."

What's Next (Why This Role)

In chapter 11, when we outlined how to effectively end your pitch, we looked at how to use your networking goals to segue out of the pitch and into conversation. While you won't use your networking goals to end your interview pitch, you will use your career goals.

You set REAL goals for your next career move in chapter 2; now it's time to incorporate them into this statement for wrapping up your elevator pitch:

> "And now I'm looking for a [*insert type of role*] for a company that values [*insert two to three values*] where I can create impact by using my [*insert two to three skills*] to [*insert first part of niche*]. This has led me to our conversation today."

Feel free to adjust this framework to make it your own—remember there's no such thing as a one-size-fits-all approach.

> **Meet Meghan:** Meghan had already developed her career goal, which was to:
>
> Take my leadership capabilities to the next level as an L&D department leader in a role that relies on my program design, coaching, relationship, and problem-solving skills, and for an organization and team that promotes consistent feedback, collaboration, and flexible scheduling.
>
> Now that she was preparing for interviews aligned with her niche, Meghan needed to incorporate that goal into the end of her elevator pitch. So, she decided to say this:
>
> And now I'm looking for an L&D leadership role for a company that encourages feedback and collaboration, where I can add value and create impact through my program design, coaching, and relationship skills to build and lead culturally aligned leadership programs, which led me to apply for this specific role and to our conversation today.

Activity

Revisit your networking elevator pitch and tweak it to align with interviewing rather than networking. Once you're satisfied with your new interview elevator pitch, it's time to practice, practice, practice. Reach out to someone you trust and ask them for feedback (this is a great time to reach out to the personal board of directors you established in chapter 10). Figure 12-2 provides a simple rubric you can share.

In addition, I highly recommend recording yourself while delivering your elevator pitch. Then, use the rubric to assess yourself. Each time you come back to it, you'll be more confident in your delivery.

Figure 12-2. Elevator Pitch Rubric

Elevator Pitch Rubric and Assessment

4 Smashing It **3** Pretty Good **2** Getting There **1** Needs Work

Criteria	Expectations	Rating	Suggestions for Improvement
Timing	• Less than 5 minutes • Doesn't feel rushed		
Confidence	• No use of qualifiers (e.g., even though, kind of, or only) • Takes ownership (uses "I" more than "we")		
Storytelling	• Story follows a logical progression • Impact is clearly stated • Clarity on skills used in each role		
Alignment	• Niche is articulated clearly • "What's next" aligns with shared experience		

Crafting Your Interview Stories

We've been taught for years that the best way to prepare for a job interview is to go through the job description line-by-line and come up with a unique example or story for each. In fact, I once believed this (and taught that method) myself! The problem is that this strategy often causes us to hyper-fixate on saying the right thing or having all the answers. And as we discussed earlier in this chapter, being overprepared in this way can cause you to lose the authenticity element of trust with your interviewer.

What if, instead of trying to memorize a different story for each line item on a job description, you only had to recall three to four stories and you could use them for multiple interviews? Feeling relieved already? I bet you are!

Why Tell Stories? It's Science!

Do you know why storytelling is so powerful? When you think about and share the moments in your career you are most proud of—when you felt like you made the most impact and value—you start to release biochemicals, including dopamine, oxytocin, and endorphins. When they're released, you start to feel happy (cue Elle Woods).

But here's the kicker, when you're sharing your story and your endorphins are ramping up, you not only start to feel happy, but the person or people on the receiving end of your story also start releasing biochemicals. The result? They feel closer and more attached to your story. Think about the last time you were truly captivated by a story—maybe it was a TED Talk, a movie, or a book you read—you were captivated not just because the content was good, but because you had an emotional response to it and your body released those biochemicals as a result.

Let's take the same approach and use our interview stories to create a biochemical connection—where we're not only connecting with the people interviewing us because we are delivering great answers, but because we're telling great stories that are compelling and make the recipient feel connected to us.

Selecting Your Stories

Thanks to all the work you've done so far in this book, you're already halfway there! Your elevator pitch provides a lot of the groundwork for your interview stories, and now you simply need to expand on them.

The first thing you want to do is select three to four moments in your career that you are most proud of accomplishing. Maybe it's sourcing and implementing a brand-new LMS that changed the way your organization delivered content, or facilitating a leadership development program that grew the confidence of first-time leaders. While you want these moments to align with your niche, it's important that you're proud of them and not just what you think someone will want to hear. (Remember, you want to trigger those biochemicals!)

Once you have selected these moments, it's time to transform them into stories. Earlier in this chapter, we discussed Frances Frei's Trust Triangle, and now we're going to touch on it again. This time, however, we're focusing on the third component of trust: logic. Why? Because when you deliver structured stories that captivate the interviewer, it allows them to trust your reasoning and judgment.

The best interview stories have four components:
- **The why** tells your audience how this situation happened and why it was important to the organization.
- **The what** shares a very high-level synopsis of the story you're about to tell. It is important to start with this rather than burying the lede until the end of your story.
- **The how** builds out the step-by-step process of how you achieved success. Be prepared to share high-level details on how the project, program, or implementation actually came to fruition. Think of this part as an expanded version of your elevator pitch.
- **The impact** shows how this moment affected the organization, learners, or clients. It's OK if you don't have specific numbers; consider the intended impact and how it helped move the needle forward.

Meet Henry: Henry was getting ready for an interview and realized he needed to brush up on his interview stories. So he thought of his proudest moment and broke down the why and the what:
- **Proud moment:** Rolling out a new graduate onboarding program
- **The why:** Low participation in new grad onboarding was increasing their overall time-to-productivity on-the-job. It was taking more than a month for new graduates to begin any independent work without managerial oversight.
- **The what:** Developed, designed, and implemented an updated new grad onboarding program designed to get new grads working semi-independently within one to two weeks of starting

When Henry started to think through the how, he identified what he had done first, which was to survey two previous rounds of new grads and their managers. In doing so, he found two main points of friction: content relevancy (everyone had to take everything) and low manager buy-in. He then crafted his story:

> I partnered with department heads, leaders, and SMEs to determine what new grads needed to know to get started on the job and what could be learned from L&D or their manager once they were on the job.
>
> I assessed all previous content, distilled it down into the "now" and "later" categories, created frameworks for SMEs to develop their own relevant content, and updated the language to be more generationally aligned. I also created a repeatable learning design framework for each new grad role, which added a personalized feel to the process.
>
> To get manager buy-in, I focused on the time to productivity metric. According to the surveys, it was taking more than 30 days, on average, for each new grad to start working on projects; managers were spending nearly 10 hours a week training their new hires.
>
> I also realized there was a communication and marketing issue because the managers didn't understand what the new grad onboarding program covered, and so were unintentionally duplicating some of the onboarding efforts. I focused on creating an internal drip marketing and communications plan to educate the hiring managers of incoming new grads eight weeks before their start date. This allowed them ample time to prepare for their new hire, review the onboarding training schedule, understand their own role in the process, and ask any questions ahead of time.

Finally, Henry reached the impact portion of his story:

> After the first new grad cohort, overall participation in the program increased by 300 percent. Instead of requiring 30 days to start working independently, new grads were taking on their own tasks in fewer than seven days. This gave hours of time back each week to managers and reduced almost all instances of duplication.

Once you've crafted your stories, you'll want to distill them into the specific skills you used. For the example, Henry's story includes these skills: onboarding, program development, content design, project management, gap analysis, assessments, SME management, learning strategy, stakeholder management, and cross-functional communication.

This last step makes it easier for you to answer any question an interviewer has regarding the job's assigned skills. In other words, Henry could use this story if his interviewer asked him to share about onboarding, project management, or learning strategy.

In the next chapter, you'll explore how to use these stories in preparation for a specific interview.

What's Next? Building Your Interview Confidence

When it comes to interviewing, the right amount of preparation coupled with clarity in your career stories is the best "cheat code" to increase your confidence. To give your interview confidence an instant boost:

- Reflect on your current preparation habits and adjust if you find yourself over preparing. Focus on being genuine rather than rehearsed.
- Write down your personal red and green flags for potential employers. Review these lists after each interview to help guide your decision making.
- Write and practice delivering your interview elevator pitch—make sure it covers your intro, origin story, career overview with added context, and what you're looking for next.
- Identify your proudest career moments, structure them into stories, and practice telling them to highlight your skills and experiences.

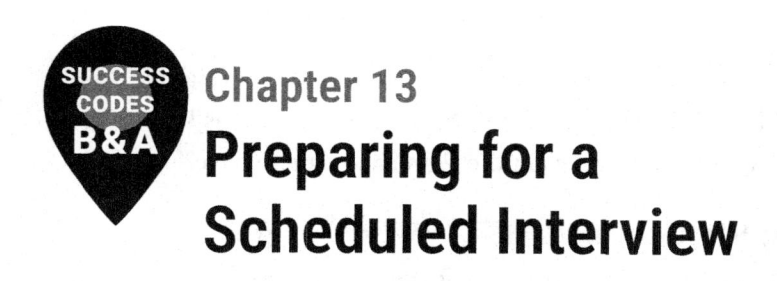

Chapter 13
Preparing for a Scheduled Interview

"An interview is not a test of knowledge, but a tool to uncover character." —Ryan Lilly

In chapter 12, we explored what it looks like to prep for interviews before they are even scheduled. The goal is to set you up for success early in the interview process and start preparing you to answer standard interview questions. But what do you focus on once you get that exciting email telling you that you've been selected for a first or next round interview?

According to Job Hunt, "The best way to succeed in an interview, most of the time, is to turn the interview from a formal question-and-answer 'grilling' into a business conversation" (Joyce 2018). You do this by asking questions tailored to each type of interview.

Interviewer Types and What to Ask Each

A huge part of interviewing is not only answering questions, but also asking them. I've said this once, and I'll say it a million times: As much as they are interviewing you, you are also interviewing them.

With that said, it's important to craft thoughtful questions that provide the answers you need to decide if this is the right role, company, or team for you. You also want to show the person interviewing you that you are interested in them, the organization, and the role.

Typically, you'll interview with four different types of people and you will need to cater your questions to each. However, before you get to the specifics, I encourage you (if time permits) to close out every interview by asking whether they have any more questions for you. Basically, you're trying to get the opportunity to fill in any blanks the interviewer may have about you. A great way to do this is by asking, "Were there any specific skills I didn't mention or walk through that you'd want the right candidate to have?"

Recruiter or HR

You'll typically talk with a recruiter or HR during the screening call, which is a brief interview to determine if your resume should be passed on to the hiring manager. The recruiter typically won't have all the information about the job's day-to-day activities, but they can offer a perspective into the company culture.

Your goal for the screening call interview is to get a better understanding of the company culture, the hiring timeline, the next steps of the interview process, and the salary range. Here are some sample questions you can ask:

- "I saw on your website that 'creativity' is one of your core values. That's one of mine too! Could you tell me more about what that looks like inside the organization?"
- "How soon are you looking to fill this role, and what interview steps could someone typically expect to go through?"
- "This role sounds incredible and I know I could bring a lot of value to it. To make sure we're both aligned, what salary range have you budgeted for this role?"

Hiring Manager

Your interview with the hiring manager will ultimately be one of the most important parts of the process. The hiring manager is looking to see if you are a fit for them and the team, and you are interviewing the hiring manager to see if you want to work with this person for 40 hours a week.

Your big-picture goals for this interview are to understand what the hiring manager needs out of the role, get a clear picture of their overall expectations, confirm you're on the same page about job responsibilities, learn about development opportunities, and uncover any challenges the role will face. Here are some sample questions to consider asking:

- What value do you see this role bringing to you and the team?
- What would success look like to you in the first 90 days? What about after the first year?
- Once onboarded, what do you expect a normal day to look like in this role?
- How do you typically work with the team on developing new skills?
- What do you think will be the biggest challenge to someone in this role?

Peers

The peer interview gives you a sense of who you will be working closely with, and what that relationship will look like. In these interviews you'll want to understand their roles, see how your role works with theirs, and learn more about team dynamics. A couple question to ask are:
- Can you tell me a little more about your role, and how you see this role working with yours?
- How do you all work together as a team?

Vice President, Director, C-Suite, or the Hiring Manager's Manager

If you've made it this far, you have made quite an impression! At this point, they're checking to see if you are a value-add to the organization or department as a whole.

Your goal in this interview is similar to the one you had with the hiring manager, but on an organizational or departmental level. Thus, you'll want to leave with an understanding of how the role influences the department or organization and how the role is perceived and is valued by the team; you'll also want a clear picture of any departmental or organizational challenges. A few sample questions to gain clarity include:
- How do you see this role influencing the departmental or organizational goals you've set?
- Where do you think this role will bring the most value?
- What do you think will be the biggest challenge to someone in this role?

> **Activity**
> If you are actively interviewing, start prepping the questions you would like to ask in your upcoming interviews. Borrow the ones from this chapter or create your own. If you are nearing the interview process, start considering the types of questions you will ask when you begin interviewing.

Answering "the Salary Question"

It's inevitable that you'll be asked about salary expectations in your screening interview. We discussed how to figure out your salary range and requirements in chapter 6 by looking at overall compensation, paid time off, healthcare benefits, and so forth. When the salary question comes up in an interview, you may feel inclined to share your range with the interviewer; however, I encourage you to ask a simple question in return before doing so: "Since it's early on in the process and I'm still understanding the full scope of the role, can you please share what you have budgeted for this role?"

This one question has earned my clients thousands, if not tens of thousands, of dollars more per year because it puts the ball back into the interviewer's court. Because most roles already have a predetermined budget and range, you could be selling yourself short or letting your possible future employer get away with hiring you below their budget if you share your numbers first. Remember, at the end of the day, organizations are businesses and even goodhearted managers are happy to save on payroll if they think they are meeting you at your expectations.

> **Meet Rebecca:** As shared in chapter 1, once Rebecca found her niche, it was off the races. Several days after applying to yet another dream L&D role, Rebecca received an invitation for an interview. On the call, the recruiter asked for her salary range; albeit nervous, Rebecca asked the recruiter to share the amount they had budgeted for the role. Turns out, it was $20,000 more per year than her target salary!

Beyond snagging an extra $20,000 a year, the higher starting salary had much bigger financial implications for Rebecca. According to The Job Sauce, "a $10K raise now is worth over $500K in career earnings if you're working for

30 more years. That figure accounts for inflation, but that's it. Earning more now makes it easier to land a higher paying job. Earning more now means contributing more to your retirement. Earning more now means having more money to invest" (Swedberg 2020). In other words, by not asking for the salary the company had budgeted, Rebecca might have left close to $1 million on the table over the course of her working career!

So, while it may be uncomfortable to push back slightly and ask for the budget instead of giving your range, ask yourself if that moment of discomfort is worth a million bucks. I'd bet a million bucks it is.

How to Spot a Learning Culture

Based on my own 15+ years of experience in L&D, as well as those of the thousands of purpose-driven people I've coached to land their dream career, I can say one thing with certainty: For L&D professionals to thrive in their next career, the organization must either already have a learning culture or highly value creating one.

A learning culture is an organizational environment that continuously encourages and supports learning and development. It's not just about having learning programs—it's about creating an ethos where learning is embedded and valued in every aspect of the organization. Could you imagine a surgeon working at a hospital that didn't value surgery? It would be hard for them to get their job done and save lives. Now, we're not surgeons and don't have a Hippocratic oath to swear by; however, an organization does have a responsibility to its employees to develop and serve them to be able to perform their jobs well. If an organization doesn't value learning, it will be nearly impossible to see the fruits of your labor.

I get asked often how to spot a toxic work environment—but the answer is that it's all relative. As we discussed in chapter 2, everyone has different needs, and how your needs are met can determine if you deem an organization toxic or not. However, you will need to learn to spot organizations that don't support a learning culture, or you'll ultimately be setting yourself up for failure. Here are 10 questions you can ask the recruiter, hiring manager, peers, or department leads to find out more:

1. Is there regular training for senior leadership to enhance their leadership and management skills?
2. Does the organization have a dedicated budget for learning and development?
3. Are employees encouraged and given time to learn during working hours?
4. Is there a structured process for employees to set and review their learning goals?
5. Are there opportunities for cross-departmental learning and knowledge sharing?
6. Does the organization reward or acknowledge continuous learning and skill development?
7. Are learning and development opportunities tailored to individual needs and career paths?
8. How does the organization regularly evaluate the effectiveness of its training programs?
9. Is there a culture of feedback and continuous improvement in place?
10. Are there mechanisms for employees to contribute to the learning content and methods used in the organization?

Some organizations have yet to develop their learning culture, so they may be looking to you to help shape it. If you are open to the task, here are a few thoughts to keep in mind and questions you can ask the interviewer for clarification:

- **Leadership involvement.** Leadership must not only endorse but actively participate in learning initiatives. Their involvement sets the tone for the entire organization.
    - *You can ask:* What is the leadership's willingness to participate in and endorse learning programs and initiatives?
- **Employee empowerment.** The organization should empower employees to take charge of their learning by providing resources, time, and support for learning activities, for example.
    - *You can ask:* What type of resources will be made available for employees in support of their learning?

- **Incorporate learning into daily activities.** Learning shouldn't be an isolated event but integrated into daily work. The organization should encourage knowledge sharing and collaboration.
  - *You can ask:* What does collaboration and knowledge sharing currently look like? How is it supported and rewarded?
- **Celebrate learning.** The organization should acknowledge and celebrate achievements in learning. This reinforces the value placed on continuous growth and development.
  - *You can ask:* How is continuous growth and development currently rewarded?
- **Customized learning paths.** Recognize that one size does not fit all in learning. The organization should tailor learning opportunities to meet individual needs and career aspirations.
  - *You can ask:* How open is the organization to personalization and sponsoring learning opportunities outside the workplace?

Interview Questions to Prepare For

We've spent most of this chapter focusing on the questions you need to ask to ensure the role and company you are interviewing for is right for you. When you embrace the mindset shift that you are interviewing them just as much, if not more, than they are interviewing you, you realize how important your questions are for finding the right fit.

That doesn't mean you won't be asked questions too. In the previous chapter, you learned about interview stories and how to use them. Now, we'll take these stories and plug-and-play key components of each into more standard interview questions.

You'll be asked three main categories of questions: behavioral and experiential, technical, and big picture. Because most interviews last between 30 and 60 minutes, you likely won't be asked all of these questions; however, you should still make sure you're prepared to answer them. Sticking to your interview stories will help make sure you're ready, without being too overprepared.

Behavioral and Experiential Questions

Behavioral interview questions focus on your past experiences to help employers gauge your behavior in relation to skills, abilities, and knowledge. An interviewer may have you describe a specific work experience using situational questions to reveal how you acted in similar situations.

Here are a few sample behavioral interview questions:
- Can you tell me about a time when you had to adapt a training program in response to feedback?
- What's your approach to evaluating the effectiveness of training or learning content?
- How would you handle resistance to training or new learning initiatives?
- What's your approach to working with stakeholders or SMEs with different opinions?
- Tell us about a time you had to make a pivot midproject.

Technical Questions

Your answers to technical interview questions are meant to showcase your technical skills. When answering these questions, it's essential to mention the tools you are most comfortable with.

Sample technical questions include:
- What tools do you use to track learning program effectiveness?
- Can you provide an example of how you've used technology to enhance employee training?
- How do you keep up with emerging technologies that are relevant to L&D?
- What other technology-based methods for delivering training have you come across or have implemented yourself?

Big-Picture Questions

Last, big-picture questions help the interviewer understand you as a whole person, including your overall motivations and general approach to work.

They allow you to showcase your authenticity and give the interviewer a glimpse of what it would be like to work with you.

Sample big-picture questions include:
- What motivates you most about the work you do?
- How do you handle conflict or disagreements in the workplace? Can you provide an example of a time you've had to resolve a work-related conflict?
- What have you done in your career that you're most proud of?
- Tell me about a time you failed. What did you learn from it?

Activity

Go through the sample questions and start to form your answers using the interview stories you came up with in the previous chapter.

AI Pro Tip

While it's impossible to prepare for every single possible interview question, an AI platform like ChatGPT may be able to help you get comfortable with the types of questions you'll be asked. Here is a sample prompt you can use:

Act as if you are the [*insert title of person interviewing you*] at [*company name*] looking to hire a [*insert job title you are interviewing for*]. This is your background: [*If you have it, you can insert information from their LinkedIn profile*].

This is the job description for the role you are hiring for: [*Copy and paste the job description*]

Here are some questions you are already prepared to ask:
- [*Insert question 1*]
- [*Insert question 2*]
- [*Insert question 3*]

What are five to seven additional questions you would ask in an interview to make sure you're hiring the right candidate?

> Once you get the answers, you may find that you need to reprompt with some additional details. When you're satisfied, you can follow up with a second prompt requesting best practices for answering those questions. For example:
>
> > Knowing your background as a [*insert title of person interviewing you*], and [*insert company name*] as an organization, what is an example of an outstanding answer for each of the above questions? What answers would make a candidate stand out to you?
>
> Remember, use this example as a guide to help you reflect on your own experiences.

What's Next? Becoming Interview-Ready

Now's the time to put all your preparation into aligned action and focus on the specific role you're interviewing for. These tips will help you prepare without over preparing:

- Develop thoughtful questions for different interview types, focusing on culture, role expectations, and challenges to ensure alignment and show genuine interest.
- Use your interview stories to create concise answers for behavioral, technical, and big-picture questions that emphasize your skills and experiences.
- Rehearse asking for the budgeted salary range instead of stating your expected range to potentially secure a higher offer.

Chapter 14
Post Interview: How to Stand Out

SUCCESS CODES A & B

"There are no traffic jams on the extra mile." —Zig Ziglar

Phew! You've finished the interview and you're ready to move along with your day—but you're not done quite yet. In this chapter, we'll cover what to reflect on after the interview, whether and how to write thank-you notes, and how to negotiate once you receive an offer for the position.

Post-Interview Reflection

After each interview, you'll want to take a few moments to reflect on the experience, how you performed, and how the interaction left you feeling. This is a great time to pull out your list of red and green flags from chapter 12 and assess your experience with those in mind. A few other reflection questions to ask yourself include:

- What are you most proud of yourself for doing in this interview?
- What three things did you do well in this interview?
- What do you want to continue doing in your next interviews?
- What would you like to improve on in your next interviews?
- How will you focus on improving in those areas?
- How will you celebrate completing this stage of the interview process?

By reflecting immediately after your interview, while the experience is still fresh in your mind, it's easier to identify what you want to keep doing and how you want to pivot.

Thank-You Notes

While your interview accounts for the majority of the hiring decision, what you do after the interview can make a big impact as well. According to a study by Topresume, 68 percent of employers and hiring managers say a thank-you note matters after a job interview; one in five interviewers even said they ruled out a candidate because they did not send a post-interview thank-you email (Editorial team 2024).

With that in mind, sending a thank-you note after each interview is non-negotiable.

A great thank-you email is an opportunity to reinforce why you're the best candidate for the role and why you are enthusiastic about the possibility of joining the team. Here's a framework you can use to write your email:

- **Restate enthusiasm.** Your opening thank you is an opportunity to share how the interview confirmed your interest in the role, company, team, and so on.
- **Revisit key themes.** This is an opportunity to revisit any themes that came up during your interview in terms of project type, challenges, role expectations, and so on.
- **Repitch yourself.** Your thank-you note serves as the exclamation point on your pitch. This is the last time you'll be able to share your value-add to the organization, team, and role.

Meet Chad: Chad had just finished a very successful interview with Michelle, the head of L&D at a large tech company. The role was aligned with his L&D niche, and the company and team values mirrored his own. Chad thought he could really add value in the L&D manager role and sent a thank-you note to help seal the deal. Here's what he wrote:

Dear Michelle,

Thank you so much for taking time out of your day to chat with me about the learning and development manager position. I was excited going into our conversation, and after hearing you share about the impact this role has the potential to make on the entire organization, I'm even more enthusiastic about the opportunity to join ABC Company.

> I particularly wanted to thank you for your candidness in terms of what you need this role to achieve, what challenges it will face, and what the reimagined business looks like. Knowing you are about to embark on scaling up your sales and sourcing team, I would be excited to bring my learning strategy, LMS sourcing and implementation, and content development experience to help increase time to productivity, decrease turnover, and get ABC Company back to $1 billion as quickly as possible.
>
> Again, I appreciate your time and would be thrilled to help you build and design the culture that's waiting around the corner for ABC Company.
>
> I look forward to hearing about next steps. Have a great rest of your week and talk soon!
>
> All the best,
> Chad

Here are a few additional tips to keep in mind when writing your thank-you note:

- **Be authentic.** Allow your writing style to mirror your personality. Your thank-you note shouldn't sound like it came from an entirely different person than the one who was interviewed. Add your own flair and personality to stand out from all the AI-generated thank-you notes they're likely getting.
- **Timing.** Don't wait too long to get your thank-you note out. A good rule of thumb is to send it the same day so you stay top-of-mind.
- **Keep it concise.** A thank-you note is not the place to request feedback or recap the entire interview. Instead, focus on gratitude and keep it to six sentences total.
- **Include a signature sign-off.** Ending your email with a signature sign-off is a great way to add an additional personal touch while remaining professional. Some examples include "All the best," "Thanks again," and my own personal sign off—"Yours in learning."
- **Send it to everyone.** From the recruiter to the hiring manager to peers, everyone should get a thank-you note.

> **Activity**
> Take some time to write a sample or template for your thank-you email. Having this baseline creates a helpful shortcut once it's time to send your note.

Negotiating Your Offer

You did it! Your hard-earned interview skills paid off and you got an offer—now it's time to negotiate! According to a 2021 recruiting and hiring survey by Brightmine HR and Compliance Centre, 90 percent of employers are willing to negotiate salary with job candidates. However, research from CareerBuilder found that only 45 percent of candidates ask for a higher salary when offered a new position.

I get it, negotiating can feel awkward—even though talking about money has become less taboo, it can still be an uncomfortable subject. However, if the organization is open to negotiating and you don't take that opportunity, you're not only leaving money on the table now, you're hurting your future earning potential. In an interview with NPR, economist Linda Babcock of Carnegie Mellon University warned that by not negotiating salary, especially in early career roles, people are "leaving anywhere between $1 million and $1.5 million on the table in lost earnings over their lifetime."

With that in mind, let's look at how to successfully negotiate your offer so you're not leaving anything on the table.

- **Shift your mindset.** It's important to remember that most organizations are expecting you to negotiate your salary. So, while it may feel awkward or scary, the person who extended your offer is probably waiting for you to come back with a counteroffer.
- **Know your number.** In chapter 6, we discussed quantifying your value. Make sure to revisit that chapter and reassess your numbers. Share your number with the person you're speaking to by saying something like, "Now that I've met with the team and understand the scope, challenges, and impact of this role, I'd be open to accepting a base salary of $100,000."

- **Give them a heads up.** Even if they are expecting you to negotiate, no one likes to be caught off guard. Send whoever extended your offer a message letting them know you received their offer, you're excited about it, and want to discuss the salary. This not only makes sure they aren't caught off guard, but it gives them an opportunity to prepare by going back to the decision maker to get a new number.
- **Get creative.** The organization may not be able to increase the salary, but don't be afraid to ask if they can make up that number through a bonus, additional equity, or more days off.
- **Express gratitude.** In any market, it's an honor and exciting to receive an offer—they chose you out of all their other applicants. Make sure they know you are grateful that they chose to bring you on board.
- **Ask open-ended questions.** Rather than saying, "Is that something you can do?" try reframing your question to be more collaborative. Consider asking open-ended questions, such as "How can we get to that number?" or "What flexibility do you have?"
- **Know when to walk away.** In most cases, you discussed salary expectations during one of your interviews prior to the offer. If not, or if the scope changed, and the number offered no longer aligns with your value, be prepared to decline politely.
- **Practice makes it easier.** It can be nerve wracking to go into these conversations, so practice out loud or with someone you trust.

What's Next? Leaving a Lasting Interview Impression

It's never too early to start thinking about how to leave an impression after your upcoming interviews. Preparing will save you time and energy.
- Create a thank-you email template that you can personalize after each interview. Include sections for restating enthusiasm, revisiting key themes, and repitching your value.
- Revisit your salary expectations and practice your negotiation script. Outline potential counteroffers (including salary, bonuses, or additional benefits) and rehearse discussing these with confidence.

Chapter 15
Navigating Career Rejection

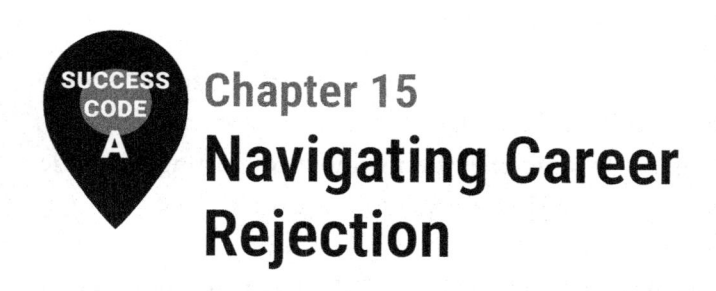

"When one door of happiness closes, another opens; but often we look so long at the closed door that we do not see the one which has been opened for us." —Helen Keller

You've likely already experienced rejection in your career—unfortunately, it's one of those things that doesn't get easier; we just get more resilient. What I've found with my coaching clients who have faced rejection (which is 100 percent of them) is that getting rejected often had nothing to do with them, and if it did, it didn't mean they were bad or wrong; it just meant that someone else had something different to offer. And sooner or later they're the one with "something different" who gets chosen over someone else.

If you've reached this chapter, you might be currently facing rejection or perhaps you're still recovering from the last one. Or maybe you're here to start building some resilience in preparation for your next rejection—which will happen. The first part of navigating career rejection is "remembering that rejection is a normal part of everyone's life," says psychologist Mark Leary, "and feeling bad about it means your brain is working the right way" (Shrikant 2023). So, if getting rejected stings—congratulations, your brain is working!

Is It Really a Rejection?

Before we start down the road of navigating career rejection, I encourage you to pause and reflect on whether it's really a rejection or not. According to Leary, *neutrality is not rejection*. "People misinterpret *ambivalence* and *neutrality* as rejection," he explains. "A lot of people see a lot more rejection than there really is" (Shrikant 2023).

If a recruiter doesn't call you back for a few days, don't jump to the conclusion they don't want to hire you. They might be sick or busy or having technical issues. If you automatically assign rejection without conducting a realistic appraisal of the situation, you set yourself up for feeling the sting of rejection, even if it hasn't happened.

So, let's ask again—Is this actually a rejection? Or are you misinterpreting ambivalence or neutrality?

Reasons for Getting Rejected

We've all been there. You left the interview on a high—you know you nailed it. You got great feedback in the moment and are optimistic about moving on to the next round or getting that offer. And then…

You get the dreaded email that says, "Thank you, but we've gone in a different direction."

While some recruiters and hiring managers may provide feedback (it always helps to ask, especially if you made it to the hiring manager round), you won't always get a reason for the rejection. While it will sting, it's important to remember that the reason you didn't get the job likely had nothing to do with you and was out of your control.

Reasons That Have Absolutely Nothing to Do With You

It's logical to immediately ask, "What did I do wrong?" and come up with a laundry list of things to change. Before you tackle that list, however, stop and reflect on the other reasons why you may not have gotten the job—the ones that have nothing to do with you. Make sure you're not inadvertently changing or stopping something that was actually working for you.

Let's look at a few reasons for getting rejected that have absolutely nothing to do with you:

- **They didn't realize they needed (or wanted) a specific skill set until they saw it (so it wasn't in the job description).** As a hiring manager, I once hired an instructional designer because of her creative writing background. It wasn't something I had originally known I

wanted or needed, but when I saw that skill listed on her resume, I realized it was a big area of opportunity for my team.
- **The role was filled internally.** Some states have laws that require job openings to be posted publicly for a specific amount of time, even if the job is already going to an internal candidate. That rejection you got from a role you thought was incredibly aligned? It might have been reserved for an internal candidate.
- **The role lost funding.** Unfortunately, it's possible for roles to lose their budgeting or funding in the middle of the hiring process. Perhaps the company didn't hit its revenue goals, the organization restructured, or someone determined the role wasn't necessary.
- **The scope of the role changed.** As applications come in, hiring managers may realize they aren't attracting the right candidate and have to change the job scope or responsibilities as a result.

Reasons Outside Your Control

Sometimes you are a factor in a rejection decision. However, that factor may be out of your control. Here are a few reasons for getting rejected that are outside your control:

- **Whoever was interviewing you was in a bad mood.** We all have bad days, and recruiters and hiring managers can have them too. If someone's bad mood throws you off your game—it's understandable why you may not be selected, even knowing their mood had nothing to do with you.
- **You were sick that day and couldn't reschedule.** Being sick is out of your control, and it absolutely influences how you function in an interview. According to Happy Neuron (Campbell 2022), you have trouble responding quickly to stimuli when you're sick—and what is an interview but constant stimuli you need to respond quickly to?
- **There were technical difficulties.** In an age when 90 percent of interviews are conducted virtually, there are bound to be technical difficulties (Sarkar 2023). Even if you prepared and tested your

internet, computer, and microphone, if they fail, it can adversely influence your interview experience.
- **You weren't a fit for their culture.** This may be a hard one to accept, but if you don't align, you don't align. According to *Harvard Business Review*, "While you may believe you can adapt to fit the environment, the hiring manager will predict your success based on how you describe your work style and preferences during the interview process. There is nothing you can do if they don't believe you'd fit in with the team or overall company culture" (Lyons 2022).
- **They went with a different candidate.** Different doesn't mean better. I had a VP-level client make it to the final round before she received a rejection that said they went with someone who had a larger global scope. While it was a bummer, she had no control over the size of her global team.
- **Your salary was mismatched.** Many of my clients have not moved on because a role couldn't meet their minimum salary requirements.

Reasons Within Your Control

As you can see, there are a lot of reasons why you may have been rejected that have absolutely nothing to do with you or were out of your control. It's safe to say that most of your rejections will fall into those two categories.

However, as a human being, you aren't completely immune to making mistakes that are within your control to fix for the next go around. Let's look at a few reasons for rejection in this category:

- **You didn't tie or translate your skills to the role.** You may have all the necessary capabilities, skills, and experience, but the recruiter or hiring manager couldn't understand how you'd apply them to this role.
- **You put the company on a pedestal.** In chapter 4, we discussed how important it is to align with the right role at the right company. If you interviewed for the sake of interviewing just so you could get a foot in the door, you may have set yourself up for rejection. Don't apply for a role that isn't aligned with what you actually want.

- **Your application was missing key details or was rushed.** According to Career Builder (2018), 77 percent of recruiters see typos or poor grammar as dealbreakers. If you're receiving a lot of immediate rejections, that is one of the first things you should look for.

> **Activity**
> Think about the last job rejection you received. What category do you think the reason for not getting an offer falls under?

How to Move Through Rejection

Whether it has nothing to do with you, was out of your control, or is in your control to change for next time, rejection will always sting. Rather than trying to move past it, I encourage you to move through it.

It's common to convince ourselves that "it's OK," even when every bone in our body is telling us otherwise. According to Nicholas Farrell, licensed clinical psychologist and a regional clinical director at NOCD, "If our definition of gaslighting is the act of invalidating one's own, true experience, then yes! It's possible for someone to gaslight themselves" (Warren 2023). The more we invalidate the pain of the rejection, the harder it becomes to see the truth of it.

To move through your rejection, you need to feel the rejection and see it for what it is. To do this, I encourage you to journal through the next eight prompts every time you face a rejection. This will give you the tools to self-reflect and reaffirm. The more you move through rejection instead of invalidating it, the more resilient you will become over time.

1. **Name the thing.** What is causing you discomfort right now?
2. **Face emotions head on.** What emotions are you really feeling and experiencing about this discomfort?
3. **Reality check.** What are you telling yourself this means about you and your future? What catastrophic predictions have you been making (conscious or subconscious)?

4. **Renew capabilities.** Despite this discomfort, what do you know to be true about the skills, abilities, and values you bring to the table? What proof do you have of this?
5. **Celebrate courage.** Where have you been courageous or stepped out of your comfort zone? What is so meaningful about that step?
6. **Healthy self-talk.** If you were your most trusted friend, how would you describe you?
7. **Learn from rejection.** What have you learned from this discomfort? What is it teaching you?
8. **Moving forward.** What more do you need to do to move through this discomfort? What does the next right step look like for you? What will you do the next time you experience this discomfort?

What's Next? Preparing for Rejection

Rejection is a natural part of the L&D career transition process. While you can't run from it, you can prepare for it by:

- Focusing on what you can control over what you can't. While you can't control most of the reasons you experience rejection, having awareness of what you can control will help prepare you for the future.
- Keep coming back to these reflections. No matter the circumstance, rejection stills stings and the sooner you go to those prompts, the sooner you can move through it.
- You're not in it alone. In chapter 10, you established a personal board of directors—you can, and should, lean on them when navigating rejections.

PART 5
Thriving in Your New L&D Role

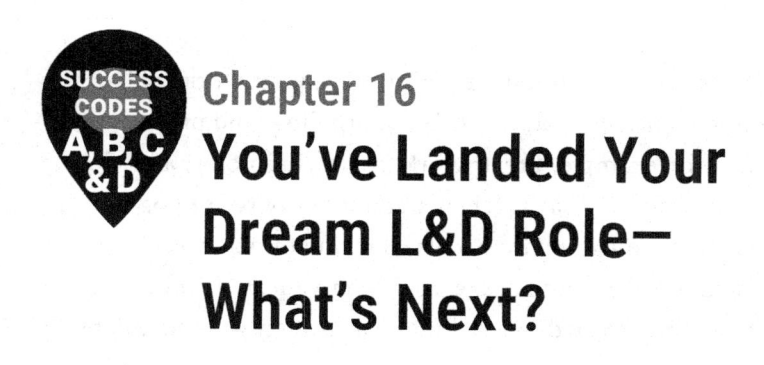

Chapter 16
You've Landed Your Dream L&D Role—What's Next?

"We do not learn from experience.... We learn from reflecting on experience." —John Dewey

Congratulations! You've landed your dream L&D role and it's aligned with your skills, interests, and values!

First things first, give yourself a moment to celebrate! It can be easy to look quickly at this major accomplishment—and then move on to what's next and start preparing for your new role. Take a breath and really marvel at your success. You made this happen and you deserve to revel in your achievements!

After taking time to celebrate, you want to give yourself the space to adjust. The come down from job seeking is real—you've just spent hours per week (on top of everything else in your life) on interviewing, networking, job applications, and so on. Now that your time is freed up, it can cause a sort of mental whiplash effect. I like to think of transitioning from one job to another (or going from being unemployed to working again) like using a dimmer rather than an on/off switch—give yourself grace as you transition into something new.

Revisit Your Motivation, Mindset, and Habits

In chapter 5, we explored your motivations, mindset, and habits. Before officially starting your new role, it's important to go back and revisit those. After making any necessary modifications, start to consider what mindsets, habits, and rituals you want to incorporate into this next chapter of your life and career. These rituals can be centered around starting your workday (such as incorporating movement, meditation, coffee, journaling, and prayer), prepping for meetings (for example, breathwork, reviewing notes, and closing out emails), ending your workday (such as signing out of technology, cleaning up your workspace, and going for a walk), kicking off your weekend (for example, my husband and I watch *Shark Tank* every Saturday morning), or any other specific moment you'd like to build consistency around and bring intentionality to.

According to research by Michael Norton (2024), Harvard Business School professor and author of *The Ritual Effect*, people "who reported using rituals to leave work behind felt more successful in separating work life from home life, in part because rituals served as a reminder to engage in self-care." Rituals not only help us during daily transitionary moments, but they also serve as reminders for how to live an intentional life alongside our career.

> **Activity**
> Revisit chapter 5 and identify some moments you'd like to start creating rituals around. They may not all stick once you start your new role, and you'll most likely form some new ones, but it's important to go in with a game plan that allows you to focus on being mindful and caring about yourself.

Onboarding Yourself With the I-OTRA Model

Now that you've checked in with the habits and motivations that will support you in this new chapter of your L&D career, you can start focusing on the role you have in your own onboarding. While many organizations have a structure to onboard you into your role, team, and company culture, those who take ownership of their own onboarding are more likely to quickly assimilate into the company culture, build strong connections, and accelerate their time-to-productivity.

According to Jessica Rivera, global onboarding expert and creator of The New Job Notebook, "There are so many resources and so much advice on how to interview and find your 'dream job' but very little about what to do once you've got it." After noticing the disconnect between what employees need when they first begin a new job and what employers are delivering, Jessica developed the I-OTRA model—an individual-centered onboarding model that provides an organized and holistic approach for employees starting a new job (Figure 16-1).

The I-OTRA model is inclusive of:

- **Individual**. It's important to remember that you, as the new hire, are an active participant in your onboarding process.
- **Organization**. Learn key information about your organization and its culture.
- **Team**. Get to know your team, co-workers, new manager, and anyone else you need to build relationships with.
- **Role**. Make sure you have clarity in the expectations and performance for your new role.
- **Ambition**. Reflect on where this new role fits into your overall career ambitions and start planning for what lies ahead.

Figure 16-1. The I-OTRA Model

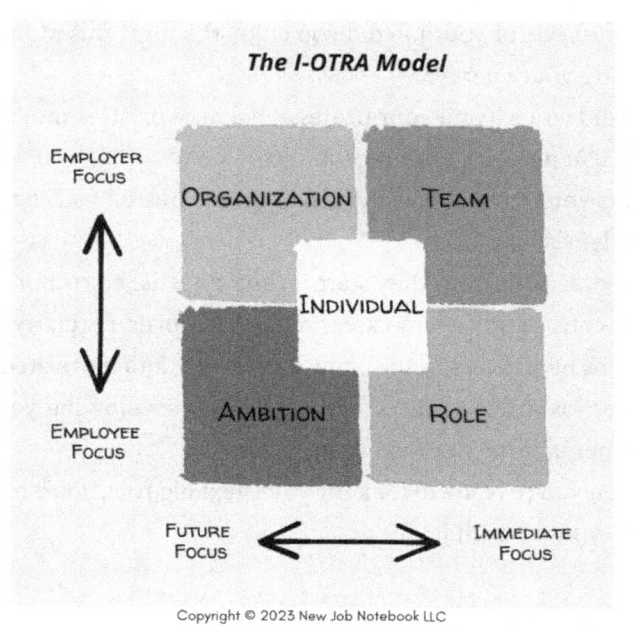

You won't have all the answers on day one (or even day 30), but by following the I-OTRA model, you become an active participant in your onboarding process, learning and gathering the information you need as you begin your new career journey.

Continuous Self-Check-Ins

Following the I-OTRA model, you'll want to continuously check in with yourself about how your new role is aligning with your legacy (which you discovered in chapter 4). A good rule of thumb is to set a monthly ambition meeting with yourself to reflect on the following:

- How do your current responsibilities align with your long-term career goals?
- What new skills or knowledge have you gained this month? (Learning and performance strategist Jess Almlie recommends spending a few minutes every day highlighting what you've learned in a Things I Learned Today or TILT journal.)
- What new skills would you like to acquire in the next month to advance your career?
- What aspects of your job did you enjoy the most this month? What is draining your energy?
- How did you expand your professional network this month? Who could you network with next month?
- How is your current role influencing your overall well-being and stress levels?

Many people wait until they start feeling dissatisfied or bored with their work to start considering a new career move. However, regularly reflecting on these questions helps you can stay focused, aligned, and motivated to continue moving closer toward your career legacy, while also allowing you to pivot or make adjustments along the way.

And when you're ready to look for your next big role, you'll have this book to help guide you through it.

Meet Murillo: In 2021, Murillo, an assistant dean for a large public university, decided he was ready for a career change into the corporate world. With a background in facilitation, learning experience design, and onboarding, he landed on a core niche inclusive of all three. Shortly after we started working together, Murillo was offered a role in his niche as a senior learning specialist and facilitator overseeing the onboarding process, program management, and delivery for more than 2,500 new hires. But landing the role was only the start of Murillo's story.

In the months after landing his new role, Murillo continued to reach out and share progress updates. He was not only thriving, but also actively focused on how he could leverage his time and resources to expand his skill set. He started reflecting on what he really enjoyed about his new role, and what was shifting the more time he spent in it. As he continued to reflect month after month, Murillo realized he was being called toward a specific career theme: L&D strategy.

So, he began to reassess his niche in terms of how it fit into his legacy of helping people grow into their potential—and set out on a development journey to increase his competencies in L&D strategy. Murillo began having higher-level conversations with the leadership team and took on additional stretch assignments to build his skills in leadership and strategic planning. He also realigned his personal brand to fit this new niche and began creating content around learning strategy to highlight what he was learning and implementing. He networked with other learning strategists and participated in opportunities to learn from real-world L&D practitioners.

Then, Murillo retraced the steps he'd taken to land that dream role in 2021. By late 2023, he was leading the entire company's learning strategy as the new senior manager of learning and development for a go-to-market revenue operations consultancy.

What's Next? Onward and Upward

You did it! Whether you landed your dream L&D role or know it's just around the corner, the work you've put into this journey of career and self-exploration is an accomplishment in and of itself. Remember, this is just one of many destinations you'll stop at on your L&D career path, and I can't wait to join you as you continue the journey. Before you close this chapter (literally with this book and figuratively as a job seeker), here are a few action items to keep the momentum flowing:

- Celebrate your achievement and transition gracefully into your new role by giving yourself time to adjust.
- Revisit and update your motivations, mindsets, and habits from chapter 5. Then, plan rituals for daily work routines.
- Actively participate in your onboarding with the I-OTRA model, which focuses on learning about the organization, team, and role while aligning with your long-term career ambitions.
- Schedule monthly self-check-ins to reflect on the alignment between your career goals, skill acquisition, job satisfaction, network expansion, and well-being.

Afterword

After supporting more than 1,000 people in their journeys to find, land, and love the L&D roles of their dreams, I had the unique opportunity to turn the tables on myself. In early 2024, I decided to take a step back from entrepreneurship and enter one of the most mystifying job markets in history. The decision to sunset major parts of my coaching business and set my sights on finding the right role at the right company did not come easy—in fact, it took me nearly seven months to even admit out loud that I was feeling pulled back to my L&D roots.

As I began to weigh the pros and cons of this pull—even going as far as interviewing at two major tech companies to get a feel for the full-time employment pool—I agonized over what direction to take my own career. Frankly, I felt imposter syndrome creeping in. How could I confidently help so many people identify their next career move but feel so frozen when it came to my own?

I had an epiphany on Christmas night. I was sitting in a Hanukkah-themed bar with my husband, and we were reflecting on the grueling year that was now behind us and our hopes for 2024. We wanted a life that centered on stability, deeper relationships, and purpose. It was at that moment I realized that, while my business had once offered me freedom, flexibility, and complete autonomy, it was no longer serving my new and evolved self. I needed something different not only in my career, but in my life.

So, in February 2024, I kicked off the search to find my next full-time role. I committed fiercely to practicing what I preach, watching my own courses, participating in my own programs, and, most special of all, using this book as a resource and to document the tools, processes, and best practices that led me to success in my own career transition. This is not to say that I didn't make many of the same mistakes I've coached my own clients not to make, such as going too far in a process I knew wasn't right for me or applying for roles I was overqualified for (and getting disappointed when I didn't get an interview). But the more I came back to the core principles discussed in this book, the easier and more aligned the process became.

After quite a few painful rejections, I landed an interview with a San Francisco-based technology company that was building out its first official learning function. (The referral came from a LinkedIn connection who had reached out to me a few years before about her own transition into L&D.) I've always told my clients that when you know, you know. As I moved through the interview process (preparing exactly as I outlined in this book), I knew I'd found the one. Thankfully, the feeling was mutual, and I landed the job. Now, I wake up every day with immense gratitude for the work I do, the people I work with, and the life this career transition has afforded me.

While the tools and processes in this book provide a precise road map for finding the right role at the right company, there's one non-negotiable piece of the puzzle for true success: faith in yourself, your abilities, and what you deserve. Even on the hardest, most doubt-filled days of my career transition, I never once faltered in my belief in myself, what I was capable of, and what I knew I deserved.

There are a lot of quotes in this book, but I'll leave you with my favorite. I carried this quote, which is attributed to Bob Proctor, with me throughout my career transition: "Both faith and fear require you to believe in something that hasn't happened yet, so why not choose faith?"

I believe in you—now it's time to believe in you too.

Acknowledgments

I wouldn't be in learning and development if it wasn't for two people who happen to share a first name. Steve Wunch showed me what it looks like and means to be a person others want to learn from. You may not have known it at the time, but your ability to capture a room, share insights, and deliver content gave me the courage to consider a career in this field.

Steven Fretwell saw something in a 24-year-old college dropout that I couldn't see in myself. The moment you called me into your office to ask why I hadn't applied for the corporate trainer role changed the entire trajectory of not only my career, but my life. Your leadership and experience showed me what *real* learning and development looked like, and you taught me the core, foundational skills I still lean on today. I owe so much of my success to you, your leadership, your foresight, and your trust.

To Genevieve, Jeanette, Emily G., and Emily C., thank you for being my L&D besties and showing me the magic that happens when smart women collaborate on big ideas. Our days together are still some of the brightest of my career. To Crystal, from starting out as your fan girl to getting the opportunity to work for you as you built LCD, this book would never have existed without your mentorship and, more importantly, your friendship. You are a true pioneer and I'm forever grateful our paths crossed and intertwined.

To my coach, Katie, for helping me clearly see all the puzzle pieces of my life and weave together a beautifully aligned picture. The best coaches have the best coaches, and your coaching fundamentally changed my life.

To the entire team at ATD for giving me a platform to share my research, skill set, and perspective—even when it went outside the norm. To Mallory, from the day we connected on LinkedIn, you have been the utmost champion of my work, making sure to connect me with people and opportunities to amplify my message. Your trust and friendship gave me the courage to expand beyond what I thought was possible for me—including writing this book! To Jack, I could not have written this book without you. Your thought partnership, editorial insights, and trust gave me the freedom and encouragement to let my personality and voice come through these pages. I can't thank you enough for seeing the value in my perspective and the opportunity to put pen to paper. To Melissa, reading through your editing comments not only made me laugh (the *Frozen* reference!) but made me feel seen and understood. Your edits took this book to a whole new level, and for that I'm so grateful. To Kay and the book marketing team, thank you for your thoughtfulness and early preparation to make this book a success—before it even hits the shelf. To Justin, Jennifer, and Morgean, thank you for seeing the value of my thought leadership and for bringing me in to work on the Talent Development Career Pathways tool. The work we did together was such a beautiful complement to the themes in this book, and I'm so grateful that it will serve as a trusted resource to our industry as it grows and evolves.

To Bridget, Jennifer, Teona, and the entire ATD conferences team, thank you for trusting me with a seat on the program advisory committee (PAC)—getting to deeply immerse myself in what top thought leaders in talent development are sharing as part of their proposals and sessions helped me keep this book future facing. To my OG PAC ladies Tonya, Myra, Nicole, Katy, and Kristin, our text thread kept me sane during the most hectic times. Thank you all for providing a safe space.

And to Lisa (even though you're no longer at ATD), thank you for reaching out and giving me my first opportunity to speak at an ATD event. I'll never forget that feeling when I got your message while on vacation. I started jumping up and down in disbelief and excitement that I'd get to share my message on the biggest talent development platform in the world. That day, you helped light a spark that's since turned into a bright flame.

It's not lost on me that none of this would be possible without the trust more than 1,000 people have put into me by choosing to engage with my courses and coaching. Whether you've purchased a course, joined a group program, or we've worked together one-on-one, the last several years of running The Overnight Trainer has been the joy of my life. Seeing your careers—and lives—transform through your effort, vulnerability, and drive has left a mark on my heart I will carry for all time. I particularly want to thank Stacey and Emma for being the first two people to see value in hiring a relatively "no-name" career coach who wanted to help folks in L&D. You two gave me the courage, hope, and energy to turn The Overnight Trainer into something more than I ever could have imagined.

To my mom, Jayne, this book (and I) wouldn't exist without you. Your passion for reading and writing etched an eternal imprint on me, and my ability to tell stories is only a fraction of the skill set you've offered the world. As a kid, I remember flipping through binders filled with the hundreds of stories you'd published throughout your career, getting lost in them and feeling so proud that my mom wrote them. Being your daughter is the best thing that ever happened to me, and I'm so proud to call such a strong, smart, and resilient woman my mom.

To my dad, David, there is no one who's come close to teaching me as much about what it means to have a strong work ethic as you. I owe my determination, grit, and perseverance to you. You showed me that even when we make mistakes, we can always make amends and get a second chance to rewrite our own narrative.

And to my sister, Molly, the bright star of our family. You have showed me what it means to find joy in every day, even while overcoming some of life's biggest obstacles. Your effervescence lights up every single room you walk into, and everyone's life you've been a part of. There's not a person who has met you who didn't fall in love with who you are and what you mean to this world.

Finally, to my husband, Brandon—thank you for being my anchor, not just while writing this book, but every single day. You are the yin to my yang, the pragmatist to my free spirit, and the roots to my garden. You never once balked when I said I was quitting my full-time job to go into the unknown market of career coaching in an incredibly niche space. Instead, you saw my potential and gave me the love, support, and encouragement to rise to the occasion. You have been by my side through the highest of highs in this business, and the lowest of lows—and always gave me the space, autonomy, and trust to make decisions (and mistakes) without judgment. Your unwavering love and belief in me fueled my fire on even the darkest of days, and I couldn't imagine doing life with anyone else by my side. I love you more than anything in the world.

Resources

Additional Book Content
Ready to explore handouts, worksheets, and resources mentioned throughout this book? Visit TheOvernightTrainer.com/book-resources to access additional, reader-only content.

ATD's Talent Development Career Pathways Tool
The Talent Development Career Pathways tool is designed to enhance your understanding of the talent development industry, to help you discover diverse job families and delve into comprehensive role descriptions so you can envision a path for your career. Use this tool to identify roles best suited to your abilities, discover the skills and capabilities you may need to build to advance your career, choose a specific role to target, and compare your current skill proficiency profile to the one needed for that role. You'll also learn about popular ATD resources designed to help you grow and develop your TD knowledge and skills as you prepare for the next step in your career. To learn more, visit td.org/career-pathways.

The Overnight Trainer Courses
Want to dive deeper into specific book topics and get step-by-step guidance on how to level up certain parts of your L&D career transition? Check out these asynchronous courses:

- **L&D Career Confidence & Clarity:** If you're struggling with finding confidence in your career transition, you're not an imposter, but you are missing something: clarity. This series will guide you to uncover your confidence and get clear on your next move!

- **L&D Career Mindset Magic:** Ready to create the ultimate mindset shift to attract your dream L&D role? Reprogram your career belief systems and develop unstoppable self and career confidence.
- **Nail Your L&D Niche:** So, you're looking for your next L&D role? With so many opportunities in such a widespread field, where do your start? By identifying your L&D niche and determining what the right role at the right company looks like for you!
- **L&D Resume Reprogram:** Tired of hearing crickets after you apply to roles? Exhausted from rewriting your resume for every job you apply to? Ready to start seeing fast results in your career transition? This course shows you how to create a single resume that will help you land the L&D role of your dreams!
- **Build Your L&D Network:** We all know your network equals your net worth, but how do you create a network you can actually leverage? In this series, you'll learn how to build an intentional, positive, and potent L&D network that works for you!
- **Uplevel Your L&D Personal Brand:** In this series you'll walk away with a niche-aligned road map to create an L&D personal brand to reach your career goals. Get ready to boost your thought leadership, optimize your LinkedIn profile, and build a brand-aligned network.
- **Create Your L&D Career Upskilling Plan:** Want to level up your own L&D personal development but don't know where to start? This course will give you the tools to conduct a skills gap analysis on yourself and create a plan to fast track your L&D career to the next level!
- **Ace the L&D Interview:** It's time to cross the finish line! This three-part course will give you aligned, practical, and repeatable strategies to show up as your best self in every interview—without having to spend hours doing so!

To learn more about these courses visit TheOvernightTrainer.com/Courses and use code BOOK20 for 20 percent off your entire course purchase.

References

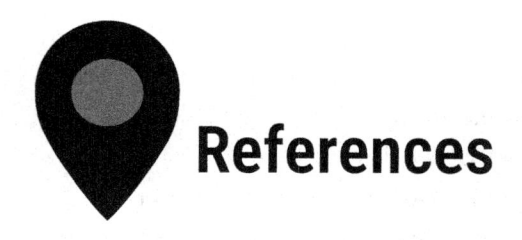

Arruda, W. 2024. "The New Formula for Successful Personal Branding." *Forbes*, May 1. forbes.com/sites/williamarruda/2024/05/01/new-formula-for-successful-personal-branding.

Ashkenas, R. 2016. "Navigating the Emotional Side of a Career Transition." *Harvard Business Review*, April. hbr.org/2016/04/navigating-the-emotional-side-of-a-career-transition.

Assaf, C. 2020. "Your Job Application Was Rejected by a Human, Not a Computer." HR Tact, October 5. hrtact.com/2020/10/05/your-job-application-was-rejected-by-a-human-not-a-computer.

Begdache, L. 2019. "Ask a Scientist: Neurons Help Explain How Our Brains Think." *Binghamton Press & Sun-Bulletin*, March 17. pressconnects.com/story/news/local/2019/03/18/ask-scientist-how-do-thoughts-work-our-brain/3153303002.

Bradshaw, R. 2024. "15 Important Networking Statistics Everyone Should Know." Apollo Technical, June 24. apollotechnical.com/networking-statistics.

Callahan, S. 2018. "Picture Perfect: Make a Great First Impression With Your Linkedn Profile Photo." LinkedIn, December 28. linkedin.com/business/sales/blog/b2b-sales/picture-perfect--make-a-great-first-impression-with-your-linkedi.

Campbell, C. 2022. "How Fevers and Colds Impact Cognition." Happy Neuron blog, October 14. news.happyneuronpro.com/how-fevers-and-colds-impact-cognition.

Career Builder. n.d. "73% of Employers Would Negotiate Salary, 55% of Workers Don't Ask." resources.careerbuilder.com/news-research/73-of-employers-would-negotiate-salary-55-of-workers-don-t-ask.

Career Builder. 2018. "Employers Share Their Most Outrageous Resume Mistakes and Instant Deal Breakers in a New CareerBuilder Study."

Press Release, August 24. prnewswire.com/news-releases/employers-share-their-most-outrageous-resume-mistakes-and-instant-deal-breakers-in-a-new-careerbuilder-study-300701888.html.

CBT (Cognitive Behavioral Therapy) Los Angeles. 2023. "The 'Act As If' Technique." CBT Los Angeles, October 14. cogbtherapy.com/cbt-blog/2013/8/26/act-as-if.

CFI Team. n.d. "Maslow's Heirarchy of Needs." Corporate Finance Institute. corporatefinanceinstitute.com/resources/management/maslows-hierarchy-of-needs.

Chu, M. 2017. "Research Reveals That Publicly Announcing Your Goals Makes You Less Likely to Achieve Them." Inc., August 8. inc.com/melissa-chu/announcing-your-goals-makes-you-less-likely-to-ach.html.

Cohut, M. 2019. "Are Our Brains Addicted to Information?" Medical News Today, June 28. medicalnewstoday.com/articles/319501.

Duperroir, B. 2023. "Managing Mental Health Through Career Transitions." October 18. LinkedIn, linkedin.com/pulse/managing-mental-health-through-career-transitions-ben-duperroir.

Dver, A. n.d. "Science Helps Us Be Kickass Confident." Innovation Women. innovationwomen.com/science-helps-kickass-confidence.

Dweck, C.S. 2006. *Mindset: The New Psychology of Success.* New York: Random House.

Editorial Team. 2024. "How to Write a Thank You Email After the Interview." Apollo Technical, June 7. apollotechnical.com/thank-you-email-after-the-interview.

Farnam Street. 2018. "Carol Dweck: A Summary of Growth and Fixed Mindsets." Farnham Street, September 16. fs.blog/carol-dweck-mindset.

Fear, C. 2022. "The Science of Setting Goals—and How to Achieve Them." ICS Learn, March 17. icslearn.co.uk/blog/study-advice/the-science-of-setting-goals-and-how-to-achieve-them.

Fennell, A. 2022. "How Long Do Recruiters Spend Looking at Your Resume?" StandOut CV, November. standout-cv.com/usa/how-long-recruiters-spend-looking-at-resume.

Fine, S., and B. Nevo. 2008. "Too Smart for Their Own Good? A Study of Perceived Cognitive Overqualification in the Workforce." *The International Journal of Human Resource Management* 19(2): 346–355.

Fish, A. 2023. "8 Tips to Better Leverage Your Network." 4 Degrees, October 12. 4degrees.ai/blog/8-tips-to-better-leverage-your-network.

Fisher, C. 2016. "5 Steps to Improve Your LinkedIn Profile in Minutes." LinkedIn blog, August 3. linkedin.com/blog/member/product/5-steps-to-improve-your-linkedin-profile-in-minutes.

Frei, F.X., and A. Morriss. 2020. "Begin With Trust." *Harvard Business Review*, May–June.

Gallup and Workhuman. 2022. "Amplifying Wellbeing at Work and Beyond Through the Power of Recognition." Gallup, October 4. workhuman.com/resources/reports-guides/amplifying-wellbeing-at-work-and-beyond.

Garber, R.I. 2013. "How Many Americans Are Scared of Networking Situations? An Infographic Showing Both Fears and Phobias for Meeting New People and Talking With Strangers." Joyful Public Speaking (From Fear to Joy), November 13. joyfulpublicspeaking.blogspot.com/2013/11/how-many-american-are-scared-of.html.

Gino, F., M. Kouchaki, and T. Casciaro. 2016. "Learn to Love Networking." *Harvard Business Review*, May. hbr.org/2016/05/learn-to-love-networking.

Gollwitzer, P.M., P. Sheeran, V. Michalski, and A.E. Seifert. 2009. "When Intentions Go Public: Does Social Reality Widen the Intention-Behavior Gap?" *Psychological Science* 20: 612–618.

Half, R. 2019. "Survey: 42 Percent Of Job Applicants Don't Meet Skills Requirements, But Companies Are Willing To Train Up." PR Newswire, March 19. prnewswire.com/news-releases/survey-42-percent-of-job-applicants-dont-meet-skills-requirements-but-companies-are-willing-to-train-up-300813540.html.

Hinkle, J. 2023. "Q&A: How Long Does an Interview Usually Last? (Plus Tips)." Indeed Career Guide, July 31. indeed.com/career-advice/interviewing/how-long-do-interviews-last.

Hobson, L. 2023. "So, You Want to Become an Instructional Designer." Dr. Luke Hobson blog, July 11. drlukehobson.com/blog1/so-you-want-to-become-an-instructional-designer.

Hreha, J. 2023. "What Is a Growth Mindset and How to Develop It in 9 Steps." Persona, August 16. personatalent.com/development/how-to-cultivate-a-growth-mindset.

JDP. 2020. "How Americans Prepare for Interviews." JDP blog. jdp.com/blog/how-to-prepare-for-interviews-2020.

Jobscan. n.d. "Why Jobscan?" jobscan.co/img/Why%20Jobscan_.pdf.

Joyce, S.P. 2018. "50+ Best Questions to Ask During Your Job Interviews (Examples)." Job Hunt, February 21. job-hunt.org/article-job-interview-questions.

LinkedIn. n.d. "About Us: Statistics." LinkedIn Pressroom. news.linkedin.com/about-us#.

Lowinger, J. 2023. "How Your Mindset Affects Outcomes." Dr. Jodie blog, February 22. drjodie.com.au/how-your-mindset-affects-outcomes.

Ludden, J. 2011. "Ask for a Raise? Most Women Hesitate." NPR, *All Things Considered*, February 8. npr.org/2011/02/14/133599768/ask-for-a-raise-most-women-hesitate.

Lyons, M. 2022. "Job Rejection Doesn't Have to Sting." Harvard Business Review, October 24. hbr.org/2022/10/job-rejection-doesnt-have-to-sting.

Martinez, M. 2023. "Mastering LinkedIn Comments: Tips, Tricks, and Strategies for Maximum Engagement & Visibility." Vengreso, November 11. vengreso.com/blog/linkedin-comments.

Maurer, R. 2021. "Most Employers Open to Negotiating Salary, Not Benefits." SHRM, February 24. shrm.org/topics-tools/news/talent-acquisition/employers-open-to-negotiating-salary-not-benefits.

McMains, S., and S. Kastner. 2011. "Interactions of Top-Down and Bottom-Up Mechanisms in Human Visual Cortex." *Journal of Neuroscience* 31(2): 587–597.

Mobilo. 2023. "9 Things to Consider When Selecting What Conference to Attend." Blog post written by ChatGPT, February 4. mobilocard.com/post/9-things-to-consider-when-selecting-what-conference-to-attend?

Nick. n.d. "What Is the Best Content for Your LinkedIn Featured Section?" Peak Profiles. peakprofiles.com/best-content-for-linkedin-featured-section.

Newport, C. 2019. *Digital Minimalism: Choosing Life in a Busy World* (New York: Portfolio).

Njombua-Fombad, A. 2021. "Why Self-Connection is Cruciual to Growth and Becoming." *Brainz*, April 7. brainzmagazine.com/post/why-self-connection-is-crucial-to-growth-and-becoming.

Norton, M.I. 2024. "The Research-Backed Benefits of Daily Rituals." *Harvard Business Review*, April 10. hbr.org/2024/04/the-research-backed-benefits-of-daily-rituals.

Parker, K., and J.M. Horowitz. 2022. "Majority of Workers Who Quit a Job in 2021 Cite Low Pay, No Opportunities for Advancement, Feeling Disrespected." Pew Research Center, March 9. pewresearch.org/short-reads/2022/03/09/majority-of-workers-who-quit-a-job-in-2021-cite-low-pay-no-opportunities-for-advancement-feeling-disrespected.

Pouget, A., J. Drugowitsch, and A. Kepecs. 2016. "Confidence and Certainty: Distinct Probabilistic Quantities for Different Goals." *Nature Neuroscience* 19:366–374. nature.com/articles/nn.4240.

Purcell, K. 2024. "Job Search Statistics: We Analyzed Nearly 1 Million Job Applications. Here's What We Learned." Jobscan, June 20. jobscan.co/blog/interview-rates-study.

Rivera, J. n.d. "New Job Notebook." Blog. newjobnotebook.com/blog.

Ruscio, A.M., T.A. Brown, W.T. Chiu, J. Sareen, M.B. Stein, and R.C. Kessler. 2008. "Social Fears and Social Phobia in the USA: Results From the National Comorbidity Survey Replication." *Psychological medicine* 38(1): 15–28. doi.org/10.1017/S0033291707001699.

Sarkar, B. 2023. "Nine in 10 Companies Still Prefer Conducting Virtual Interviews: Survey." *The Economic Times*, July 28. economictimes.indiatimes.com/jobs/hr-policies-trends/nine-in-10-companies-still-prefer-conducting-virtual-interviews-survey/articleshow/102192535.cms.

Shrikant, A. 2023. "Here's Why Rejection Is Actually Good for Your Brain, According to a Psychologist." CNBC Make It, February 17. cnbc.com/2023/02/17/why-rejection-is-good-for-your-brain-according-to-a-psychologist-.html.

Silva, L. 2023. "The Mental Health Benefits of a Clean Home." Newport Healthcare, January 26. newporthealthcare.com/resources/press/clean-home-benefits.

Skees, C. 2023. "If You Want to Grow Your Network…" LinkedIn post. linkedin.com/posts/activity-7102266143209377792-KKCq.

Smith, M. 2023. "This Common LinkedIn Mistake Can Hurt Your Chances of Landing a Job Offer—How to Avoid It." CNBC Make It, August 31. cnbc.com/2023/08/31/career-expert-avoid-this-common-linkedin-mistake-when-job-hunting.html.

Stuifbergen, A.K., H. Becker, G.M. Timmerman, and V. Kullberg. 2003. "The Use of Individual Goal Setting to Facilitate Behavior Change in Women With Multiple Sclerosis." *Journal of Neuroscience Nursing* 35(2): 94–99, 106. pubmed.ncbi.nlm.nih.gov/12795036.

Sulat, S. 2021. *Agile Unemployment: Your Guide to Thriving While Out of Work* (New York: Re: Working).

Swedberg, S. 2020. "Value of a Single, Significant Raise." The Job Sauce, June 10. thejobsauce.com/value-of-a-single-significant-raise.

SWNS. 2023. "Job-Seekers Report Feeling Underqualified for Prospective Jobs: Poll." *New York Post*, March 31. nypost.com/2023/03/31/job-seekers-feel-underqualified-for-prospective-jobs-poll.

Tay, L., and E. Diener. 2011. "Needs and Subjective Well-Being Around the World." *Journal of Personality and Social Psychology* 101(2): 354–365. doi.org/10.1037/a0023779.

Warren, E. 2023. "Can You Gaslight Yourself? A Therapist's Take." NOCD, September 21. treatmyocd.com/what-is-ocd/info/related-symptoms-conditions/can-you-gaslight-yourself-a-therapists-take.

Wood, A.M., S. Joseph, and J. Maltby. 2008. "Gratitude Uniquely Predicts Satisfaction With Life: Incremental Validity Above the Domains and

Facets of the Five Factor Model." *Personality and Individual Differences* 45(1): 49–54.

Zak, P.J. 2015. "Why Inspiring Stories Make Us React: The Neuroscience of Narrative." *Cerebrum*, February. pmc.ncbi.nlm.nih.gov/articles/PMC4445577.

Zintz, S. 2018. "Effectiveness of a Growth Mindset in Education." Northwestern College, Iowa, Master's Thesis and Capstone Projects, May.

Index

Page numbers followed by *f* and *t* refer to figures and tables, respectively.

A

ABCDs (career success codes), 11–17, 16*t*
Abrahami, Janel, 119, 123
A/B testing, 94, 152
"act as if" behavioral strategy, 38
action-led mindset model, 38*f*
Agile Unemployment (Sulat), 81
Alexis, Sabrina, 79
alignment, 14–16
    checking in on, 206
    clarity and, 10
    in digital spaces, 66–67
    in elevator pitches, 167
    finding, 58
    in goal setting, 63
    in interview readiness, 186
    in physical spaces, 65–66
    sweet spot of, 81–84
    in timelines, 31, 33
    of values, 54, 166
alignment success code, 10, 14–15
Almlie, Jess, 204
Amara, Heather Ash, 1
Amazon, 110
American Confidence Institute, 35
Annan, Kofi, 49
Apple, 110
applicant tracking systems (ATS), 95
Arruda, William, 109
artificial intelligence (AI), 5, 47, 101, 114, 121, 152, 185, 189
Ashkenas, Ron, 132
Assaf, Christine, 95
ATD's International Conference & EXPO, 145
auditing, 63, 65, 67, 137
authenticity, 93, 109, 125, 164, 171, 185

B

Babcock, Linda, 190
behaviors
    "act as if" strategy of, 38
    and core values, 41–42
    interview questions about, 184
    and origin stories, 154–155
    as red flags, 166
    root-source thoughts effect on, 36–37
    and self-awareness, 74
boundaries, 74
belonging needs, 20, 23, 25, 133
bonuses, 23, 88, 108, 191
Boolean searches, 55–56, 142
boundaries, 74
branding. *See* personal branding
branding success code, 10, 14–15

brand pillars, 110–111, 112, 114, 118–119, 123, 125, 125. *See Also* personal branding
Brightmine HR and Compliance Centre, 190

C

calls to action (CTAs), 108
CareerBuilder, 190, 197
career clarity funnel, 41, 41*f*
career coaching, 20, 83, 101, 135–136
Career Golden Circle, 51*f*, 53–57, 56*f*, 86–87, 113
career leveling, 88–89
career mindset pillars. *See* 4 Rs of mindset reprogramming
career success codes (ABCDs), 11–17, 16*t*
Carnegie Mellon University, 190
cash allowances, 88
Chapman, Gary, 23
ChatGPT, 47, 101, 114, 185
cheerleaders, 147–148
Cisco Meraki, 152
clarity. *See also* confidence
  in abilities, 39–41
  and alignment, 10
  in career level, 88
  in core values, 41
  in future visions, 36–39
  and interview confidence, 175
  and job security, 22
  and networking, 137
  practice of, 48
  and uncertainty, 35
Clear, James, 70
coaches, 147–148

coaching
  career, 20, 83, 101, 135–136
  as community, 10
  leveraging, 55, 131
  self-, 70, 72–73, 76
community success code, 10, 13, 15, 18
conferences, 24, 47, 145. *See also* events
confidants, 147–148
confidence, 35–48. *See also* clarity
  in abilities, 39–41
  and core values, 41
  in elevator pitches, 167
  in future visions, 36–39
  and interests, 42
  in interviews, 175
  personal development plans for, 46–48
  and skills, 42–43
  upskilling for, 43–44
Confidence Is a Choice (Dver), 35
connection prompts, 151–153
connectors, 147
conscious commitment, 68–69, 74
content creation, 121–124
content engagement, 119–121
core values
  of companies, 1
  components of, 41
  defining, 54
  in L&D niches, 54, 188
  in personal branding, 111
  reflecting on, 125
cover letters, 105–108
  calls to action in, 108
  challenges in, 106–107
  climax of, 107–108

main character in, 106
and skills-chronological resumes, 99
as trailers, 105–106
CTAs (calls to action), 108

D

decision making, 41–42, 99, 111, 148, 175
development
    leadership, 135, 148
    in learning environments, 181–183
    personal, 11, 14, 46–48
    professional, 11, 13, 15, 43, 81
    self-, 46
    of skills, 5, 182
Dewey, John, 201
Digital Minimalism (Newport), 66
digital spaces, 66–67
Duperroir, Ben, 133
Dver, Alyssa, 35
Dweck, Carol, 61

E

elevator pitches, 153–158
    best practices for, 157–158
    career overviews in, 155
    conclusion of, 155–156
    confidence in, 167
    four-part networking, 153*f*
    in interview preparation, 166–167
    intros to, 153–154
    origin stories in, 154–155
    rubric for, 171*f*
    storytelling in, 167
    structure of, 168
    timing of, 167
empathy, 164

employee resource groups (ERGs), 23
equity compensation, 88
equivalent experience, 83–84
esteem needs, 24, 26
events, 47, 129, 130, 132, 144, 145. *See also* conferences
experience value, 87–88
experts, 147–148

F

Farrell, Nicholas, 197
Fish, Alex, 133
The Five Languages of Appreciation in the Workplace (Chapman), 23
flipped mentality, 93–94
flipped model of self-coaching, 72
Fogg, BJ, 70
4 Rs of mindset reprogramming, 62–75
full-circle approach to needs, 21*f*, 24–26
future bosses, 135
future peers, 135

G

Gallup, 23
gap assessments. *See* skills and interest gap assessments
Garvey, Marcus, 35
The Global Learning and Development Community, 144
goal-aligned questions, 158–160
goal setting
    intentions before, 26–28
    needs-first approach to, 20–28
    REAL vs. SMART, 28–30
    timelines for, 30–33
Gollwitzer, Peter, 29

gratitude, 74, 189, 191, 207
green flags, 24, 163, 165–166, 175, 187
growth mindset, 61–62, 76

H
habits. *See also* hobbies
    commitment to, 68–69
    prioritizing, 67–68
    reconnecting to, 74
    revisiting, 201
    and self-image, 41
    of self-love, 76
    sustainable, 11
habit stacking, 70
habitual systems and structures, 68
Harvard Business Review, 196
Harvard Business Review Leaders Handbook (Ashkenas), 132–133
Harvard Business School, 98, 164, 202
high urgency, high time, low preparedness timeline, 31–32, 32*f*
hobbies, 67–68, 69, 70, 74, 76, 103. *See also* habits
Hobson, Luke, 117–118

I
Indeed, 55
intentions
    in digital spaces, 66
    in goal audits, 63–64
    before goal setting, 26–30
    habits for, 68
    and intrusive thoughts, 72–73
    for networking, 131, 134, 139–140, 160
    in physical spaces, 64–65
    prioritizing, 67

    recommitting to, 63, 67
    reconnecting to, 74
    self-coaching for, 70
    shifting, 67
interests. *See also* skills
    alignment of, 10, 26, 81
    assessing, 43–44
    in content creation, 123
    in cover letters, 108
    in goal setting, 111
    in golden circle, 86
    and green flags, 166
    identifying, 42, 52–53, 59
    in interviews, 177, 186
    in L&D niches, 49–50, 92, 93
    in networking situations, 158, 160
    in niche statements, 142
    in personal development plan, 46
    in personal stories, 114
    on resumes, 103
    and roles, 55
    shifting, 48
    showcasing, 14
    in thank-you notes, 188
    in vicious application cycle, 40
International Journal of Human Resource Management, 79
interview confidence, 175
interviewer types, 177–180
interview preparation, 163–175
    and career overviews, 168–170
    confidence building for, 175
    elevator pitch in, 166–167
    over-preparation in, 164
    for post-interview, 164
    questions for, 183–185

red and green flags in, 165–166
for scheduled interviews, 177–186
stories for, 171–175
interview stories, 171–175. *See also*
origin stories; storytelling
I-OTRA model, 202–204, 203*f*

J
Job Hunt, 177
job offers, 190–191
Jobscan, 112

K
Keller, Helen, 193

L
Ladders, 97
Lattimer, Christina, 109
L&D Cares, 144
The L&D Collective by 360Learning, 144
The L&D Forum, 144
L&D niches, 49–59
bosses in, 135
core values in, 54, 188
definition of, 49
finding, 50–54
in flipped mentality, 93–94
identifying, 131
interests in, 49–50, 92, 93
and learning goals, 132
legacies in, 50–51
market value of, 86–87, 89
in profile statements, 96, 154
proof of concept in, 57–58
roles in, 55–56
skill and interest identification in, 52–53

skills in, 49–50
statements of, 59
steps toward, 52
three parts of, 50*f*
using, 54–56
L&D Shakers, 144
leadership development, 135, 148. *See also* development
lean networking goals, 132–133, 159
learning cultures, 181–183
learn networking goals, 132, 156, 159
Leary, Mark, 193
legacies, 50–51, 59, 204, 205
leverage networking goals, 131–132
lifestyle preferences and changes, 80
Lilly, Ryan, 177
LinkedIn
advanced functions of, 117–124
chatting on, 57
as community, 10
connections in, 130, 139–140
content engagement on, 119–121
free groups on, 143
new connections in, 142–143
personal notes on, 152
searching on, 55, 142
LinkedIn profiles, 10, 59, 95, 112–124, 185
logic, 164, 173
Lowinger, Jodie, 37
low urgency, low time, low preparedness timeline, 32
LRN DEV REV, 144

M
market value, 86–89
Maslow's Hierarchy of Needs, 20, 21*f*, 25

Medical News Today, 155
medium urgency, medium time, high preparedness timeline, 32–33
mentors, 2, 24, 135, 147
"me-time" activities, 27, 68–69
micro-emotions, 71, 73
micro-goals, 27–30, 33
mindfulness, 73–74, 131, 202
    resetting, 76
mindsets, 61–76
    action-led model of, 38*f*
    fixed, 61
    growth, 61–62, 76
    marketing, 91
    and personal development, 11
    reprogramming, 61–62
    revisiting, 202
    self-development, 46
    and self-perception, 38
    shifting, 190
    and synaptic pruning, 37
Mobilo, 145
motivators, 135

N

needs-first approach to goal setting, 20–28
    belonging, 23
    esteem, 24
    full-circle approach to, 24–26
    physiological, 22
    security, 22
    self-actualization, 24
network ecosystems, 139–149
    building, 139–146
    connection prompts in, 151–152
    connections of connections in, 141–142
    current connections in, 141
    events and conferences for, 145
    free online groups in, 143
    leveraging and maintaining, 148–149
    and LinkedIn, 142–143
    memberships and associations for, 145–146
    personal board of directors (PBOD) in, 146–148
    structured communities in, 144
networking
    goals for, 131–133
    house metaphor for, 136–137
    impactful conversations in, 151–160
    lean goal answers for, 132–133
    learn goal answers for, 132
    leverage goal answers in, 131–132
    reciprocity in, 133–134
    rule of thirds in, 134–136
    3 Ls of, 129–137
networking conversations, 151–160
    connection prompts for, 151–153
    elevator pitches in, 153–158
    goal-aligned questions in, 158–160
The New Job Notebook blog, 202
Newport, Cal, 66
niche-aligned application strategies, 94*f*
niche-aligned resumes, 91–105
    cardinal rules for, 94–95
    education in, 101–102
    experience in, 97–101
    extra information in, 103

flipped mentality for, 93–94
headers in, 95–96
and marketing mindset shifts, 91–92
one-and-done methodology for, 92–93
parts of, 95–102
profiles statement in, 96–97
technical skills in, 102
niche statements
in cover letters, 106
creating, 54–55
in elevator pitches, 153–154, 160
interests in, 142
in LinkedIn profiles, 58, 113
in LinkedIn searches, 142–143
skills in, 142
use of, 59
Njombua-Fombad, Antoinette, 74
NOCD, 197
Norton, Michael, 202

O

Offbeat, 144
office walk-by test, 52
onboarding, 1–2, 55, 202–204
$100 rule, 105, 108
origin stories, 154–155, 168. *See also* interview stories; storytelling

P

paid time off (PTO) policies, 22
PDPs (personal development plans), 11, 12, 14, 46–47
Perplexity, 47
personal board of directors (PBOD), 146–148

personal branding, 109–125. *See also* brand pillars
in Career Success Code, 10
content creation in, 121–124
content engagement in, 119–121
core values in, 111
getting started with, 110–111
in L&D niches, 13
leveraging, 125
LinkedIn functions for, 117–124
in LinkedIn profiles, 14–15, 59
portfolios in, 117–118
recommendations in, 115–116
of SMEs, 33
in vicious application cycle, 40
work samples in, 117–118
personal brand spectrum, 110*f*, 112
personal development, 11, 14, 46–48. *See also* development
personal development plans (PDPs), 11, 12, 14, 46–47
Pew Research, 24
physical spaces, 64–66
physiological needs, 22, 25
placement, 79–89
portfolios, 10, 40, 95, 117–118. *See also* work samples
post-interview period, 187–191
negotiating during, 190–191
reflection in, 187
thank-you notes in, 188–189
preferred qualifications, 82
Princeton Neuroscience Institute, 64
professional development, 11, 13, 15, 43, 81. *See also* development
profile statements, 96–97, 99
profit sharing, 88

proof of concept, 57
Psychology Today, 70

Q

qualification Goldilocks effect, 79–81
qualifications
    in job descriptions, 83
    preferred, 82
    reflecting on, 88–89
    required, 82
    on resumes, 97
quantifying value, 84–88
    of experience, 87–88
    and market value, 86
    for salary, 85–86

R

REAL goals, 28–33
recognition, 24, 26
recommitting, 62–67
reconnecting, 41, 62, 73–76
recruiters
    applicant tracking systems as, 95
    content creation for, 121
    cover letters for, 105
    as interviewers, 178
    profile statements for, 96
    questions for, 181–182
    rejection from, 194–197
    skills-chronological hybrid resumes for, 97
    skills listings for, 115
    thank-you notes for, 189
    use of LinkedIn profiles by, 112
red flags, 163, 165–166, 175, 187
rejection, 193–198
    moving through, 197–198
    preparing for, 198
    reasons for, 194–197
    from recruiters, 194–197
reprioritizing, 67–70, 70
    best practices for, 69
    and conscious commitment, 68–69
    of habitual systems and structures, 68
    and hobbies, 69
required qualifications, 82
results-to-thoughts cycle, 72f
resumes
    bullet points on, 99–100
    cardinal rules for, 94–95
    education on, 101
    interests on, 103
    niche-aligned (*See* niche-aligned resumes)
    qualifications on, 97
    scannability of, 103
    skills-based, 97
    skills-chronological hybrid, 97–98
    technical skills on, 102
rewiring, 28, 62, 70–73
The Ritual Effect (Norton), 202
rituals, 201–202
Rivera, Jessica, 202
role models, 148
root-source thoughts, 36–37, 37f
rule of thirds, 134–136

S

safe spaces, 64–67, 210
salaries
    calculating, 89
    and experience value, 87–88
    in interview questions, 178, 180–181, 186

three-pronged approach to, 61*f*
in value quantification, 85–86
Salary.com, 86–87
salary ranges, 61*f*, 84–85, 87–89, 178, 180, 186
scheduled interviews
    interviewer types in, 177–180
    and learning cultures, 181–183
    preparation for, 177–186
    preparing questions for, 183–186
    salary questions in, 180–181
security needs, 22, 25
self-actualization needs, 24, 26
self-awareness, 74
self-care, 11, 74, 202
self-check-Ins, 204–205
self-coaching, 70, 72–73, 76
self-development mindset shift, 46
self-forgiveness, 74
self-image, 41–42
self-love wheel, 74–75, 75*f*
severance packages, 22
Shark Tank, 202
Sinek, Simon, 51, 86
skills
    alignment of, 10, 26, 81
    analysis, 156–157
    assessing, 43–44
    in content creation, 123
    in cover letters, 108
    in goal setting, 111
    in golden circle, 86
    and green flags, 166
    identifying, 42, 52–53, 59
    in interviews, 177, 186
    in L&D niches, 49–50, 92, 93
    in networking situations, 158, 160
    in niche statements, 142
    in personal development plan, 46
    in personal stories, 114
    on resumes, 103
    and roles, 55
    shifting, 48
    showcasing, 14
    technical, 102, 184
    in thank-you notes, 188
    transferable, 43, 50
    in vicious application cycle, 40
skills and interest gap assessments, 15, 43–44, 45*t*, 47, 48
skills-based resumes, 97. *See also* resumes
skills-chronological hybrid resumes, 97–98. *See also* resumes
SMART goals (specific, measurable, achievable, relevant, and time-bound), 19, 28–30
"So You Want to Become an Instructional Designer" (Hobson), 117
Stanford University, 61
storytelling, 106, 113, 118, 166–170, 172, 192. *See also* interview stories; origin stories
subject matter experts (SMEs), 33, 174, 184
Sulat, Sabina, 81
synaptic pruning, 36–37

T

thank-you notes, 188–189
thoughts-to-results cycle, 71*f*
3 Ls of networking, 129–137
    lean, 132–133
    learn, 132
    leverage, 131–132

TILT journals, 204
timeframes, 17–18, 26, 28–34
timelines, 30–34, 31–32, 32, 32–33, 32f
Topresume, 188
The Training, Learning, and Development Community, 144
transferable experience, 83

U
underemployment, 5, 81
unemployment, 5, 31, 81, 201
University of California, Davis Internship and Career Center, 153
University of Central Florida, 1
upskilling, 11, 15, 31, 43–44, 46–47

V
value alignment, 54, 166
value quantifying, 84–88, 190
vicious application cycle, 39–40, 40f

W
WITHIN, 74
Workhuman, 23
Work-life harmony, 80, 89
work samples, 117–118, 164. *See also* portfolios
Wunch, Steve, 2

Z
Zeldin, Theodore, 151
Ziglar, Zig, 187

About the Author

Sarah Cannistra is a learning and development leader and career coach dedicated to helping others grow in the field. She began her career in real estate sales, where she thrived in understanding clients' needs and guiding them to their perfect homes. As she moved into management, Sarah discovered an even greater passion—coaching and developing people. She built training programs and learning resources for her team, finding deep fulfillment in their growth. Her career path shifted entirely when she attended a leadership development session and realized that facilitating learning was the work she was meant to do. That moment led to her first role in L&D—offered to her on the spot—despite having no formal background in the field.

Less than two years later, Sarah became the director of corporate training for an organization of more than 2,500 employees. Since then, she has led the learning function at five organizations across real estate, retail, tech, consulting, and healthcare. She's created hundreds of training programs, hired more than 100 L&D practitioners, and served more than 20,000 learners. Since 2020—through coaching, courses, and communities—she has helped more than 1,000 people transition into L&D careers, guiding them to find, land, and grow in roles they love.

Sarah is also the host of *The L&D Career Club Podcast*, a top 200 career podcast dedicated to helping professionals break into and thrive in the L&D field.

She lives in Austin, Texas, with her husband, Brandon, and their two dogs, Susie and Gail.

About ATD

The Association for Talent Development (ATD) is the world's largest association dedicated to those who develop talent in organizations. Serving a global community of members, customers, and international business partners in more than 100 countries, ATD champions the importance of learning and training by setting standards for the talent development profession.

Our customers and members work in public and private organizations in every industry sector. Since ATD was founded in 1943, the talent development field has expanded significantly to meet the needs of global businesses and emerging industries. Through the Talent Development Capability Model, education courses, certifications and credentials, memberships, industry-leading events, research, and publications, we help talent development professionals build their personal, professional, and organizational capabilities to meet new business demands with maximum impact and effectiveness.

One of the cornerstones of ATD's intellectual foundation, ATD Press offers insightful and practical information on talent development, training, and professional growth. ATD Press publications are written by industry thought leaders and offer anyone who works with adult learners the best practices, academic theory, and guidance necessary to move the profession forward.

We invite you to join our community. Learn more at **TD.org**.